David Ben Senet is an international author on the subjects of ancient healing, angels and reincarnation. His current works are available in several languages worldwide. He is also a past-life therapist and spiritual teacher. He resides in Saskatoon, Canada, with his wife, Carol.

This book is dedicated to my wife, Carol. She is my soulmate and inspiration. Her encouragement allowed me to write *The Scroll of Jesus*.

David Ben Senet

THE SCROLL OF JESUS

AUSTIN MACAULEY PUBLISHERS™

LONDON • CAMBRIDGE • NEW YORK • SHARJAH

A CIP catalogue record for this title is available from the British Library.

ISBN 9781528911337 (Paperback)
ISBN 9781528911344 (E-Book)

www.austinmacauley.com

First Published (2018)
Austin Macauley Publishers Ltd
25 Canada Square
Canary Wharf
London
E14 5LQ

I would like to acknowledge the valuable information I received by reading the books *The Secret Gospel of Thomas* and *The Gnostic Gospels*. Elaine Pagels is the author of these works. Both books proved invaluable in my research.

Also, *The Gospel of Judas* was enlightening. This gospel contains the secret account of the revelation that Jesus spoke in conversation with Judas Iscariot. It holds a spiritual message.

Author's Note

The historian, Flavius Josephus, writes about King Herod the Great in his book, Antiquities. He describes the disease that Herod suffered from along with his eventual death. Many of the violent crimes that King Herod is responsible for are detailed in this ancient book. Herod was very paranoid and became even more so near the end of his long reign. He murdered one of his wives (Mariamne) and three of his sons along with executing countless people. For a few years prior to his death, he suffered with open sores on his legs. Maggots filled these sores and had to be removed by his physicians. He died from chronic kidney disease and gangrene.

When Herod became paranoid, he would have someone killed. He would then become depressed. As his depression ended, he would build, build and build. He repeated this cycle over and over during his lifetime.

Many biblical historians do not believe that King Herod ordered the Slaughter of the Innocents in Bethlehem. This event is only mentioned in the Gospel of Matthew and not in any other Gospels. Even Flavius Josephus, who wrote in detail about King Herod including his numerous murders, does not mention this event.

This event may have been written in the Gospel of Matthew in order to fulfill an Old Testament prophecy spoken by the prophet Jeremiah. Modern bibliographers do not believe this event ever happened. I am inclined to agree with them.

Historians and archeologist are not entirely certain of the date of King Herod's death. Most believe it was 4 BC. However, there was a conjunction of the planets Jupiter and Venus in 2 BC. This celestial event may have given rise to the Star of Bethlehem story mentioned in the bible. For this reason, many historians and archeologists believe that King Herod died shortly after this celestial occurrence around 1 BC which makes sense.

Jesus had a large and extended family including many siblings and cousins. I believe he had a twin brother who was named Judah Thomas. One of the Gnostic Gospels mentions this. The sighting of Jesus at the Sea of Galilee after his crucifixion is entirely plausible if his twin brother Judah died on the cross in his place. Jesus would have then returned to Galilee to be with his family and disciples.

When I did research on the twelve disciples of Jesus, I found all of them to be very real people. They all lived, worked and eventually died. Research shows where some of them were born, where they lived and what they did. Even the dates when most of them died are recorded. This makes them very real people to me.

Pontius Pilatus was also a very real historical figure. The Pilate stone, a damaged block of carved limestone, was discovered at the archeological site of Caesarea Maritima in 1961. It mentions the name Pontius Pilatus. He was the governor or prefect of the Roman province of Judea from AD 26–36. He returned to Rome in 36 AD and may have committed suicide around 38 or 39 AD.

As a Jewish male, Jesus would have been married. In the Gnostic Gospel of Phillip, a text states that Jesus would often kiss Mary on her mouth. Jesus also explains in this Gospel why he loves Mary more than his other disciples. Other Gnostic Gospels describe the close relationship that Mary Magdalene and Jesus had. She is even referred to as beloved.

Jesus as a Master Teacher had both male and female disciples and followers. The original twelve disciples were the inner members. Many other followers and disciples were also a part of the movement.

The wife of Pontius Pilatus who was not named at that time was believed to have been a student of Jesus. So was the rich merchant Joseph of Arimathea who played a pivotal role in this narrative.

The three wise men or Magi were followers of the religion of Zoroastrian. They would have been astrologers and astronomers. Celestial events such as the conjunction of the planets Jupiter and Venus were considered very special. They often heralded the birth of a famous person.

Publius Sulpicius Quirinius, Roman governor of Syria, initiated a census of Judea upon the imposition of direct Roman rule in 6 AD. The gospel of Luke places the census within the reign of King Herod the Great who died ten years earlier. Most scholars believe the author of Luke simply made a mistake.

The master teacher and healer Jesus was a very real man who walked this earth almost two thousand years ago. His message of love still gives us hope even today.

Chapter One
Cairo, March 2016

David Benjamin, an experienced archeologist, leaned back from the wooden desk where the ancient scroll lay open. He was an expert in several ancient languages including Aramaic, Coptic, Greek and Hebrew.

He rubbed his tired eyes and yawned deeply. The noise of Cairo filtered in to his rented apartment. It was early evening and the sounds were starting to decrease as the work day in this Egyptian city came to an end.

David opened a nearby window for fresh air and felt the breeze on his face. The temperature had been cooler for the last few days which was a pleasant reprieve from the heat that Cairo was known for.

A few cries, some laughter and the occasional horn from a vehicle drifted in from outside. He found this comforting as he leaned forward to re-examine the old scroll. "Hmm. Yes, the style of writing, the age of the scroll and the patina all help to confirm this as a real document," David mumbled under his breath. Talking to himself was a habit he had formed years ago due to the countless hours of solitude during research on ancient documents.

Archeologists, sometimes, had to deal with unethical and questionable characters. The black market trade in antiquities was rampant throughout this part of the world. Fortunately, David had business dealings with an artifacts dealer here in Cairo who was somewhat honest and trustworthy.

He let his mind wander back a week ago to the morning he received a cell phone call from Ahmed Fariz, the merchant specializing in ancient scrolls and documents who was his long time business associate. Ahmed could read Egyptian Hieroglyphs as well as some Aramaic, Coptic, Latin and Greek.

He had inherited his father's business and studied these ancient languages while working with his late father. He had also been university educated in Great Britain as a young man. This made him a valuable business associate in David's eyes.

David Benjamin answered his cell phone on the third ring, "Hello. Doctor Benjamin speaking."

"David. It's me, Ahmed. I have something exciting I need to show you. I have just acquired something special, an ancient scroll written in Aramaic."

The archeologist's eyes went up a bit as he heard the news, "Aramaic. Really?"

"Yes. I read through the scroll with my limited understanding of the language. From what I could comprehend, this is a story about Jesus. This is an amazing find. During the two nights I stayed up late and struggled through it, I kept thinking of you. Hence the call, my friend. You need to come to my shop as soon as possible. When can you come?"

"Hmm," thought David for a moment. "I can be there around two this afternoon."

Ahmed Fariz's store was located on a narrow street that had an open air market nearby and many shops everywhere. Tourists would often shop here for souvenirs and other items along this busy street.

David paid the taxi driver, and stepped out into the edge of the busy and noisy market. He walked purposefully through it, entered the narrow street full of pedestrians and proceeded to Ahmed's antique shop just up on the right hand side.

When he walked into the place, a small bell over the door jingled. In seconds, a bearded face peered out from the opened door in the back of the crowded store. A smile lit up the face of Ahmed the dealer as he spotted David standing there.

It took the archeologist a few moments to let his eyes adjust to the darkened interior. Then he took a few steps forward and hugged the antiques dealer as they met in the middle of the room. They had known each other for years. Ahmed had always been fair in his business dealings with David so there was a good chance an agreement could be made, if the document was really that important.

The large room of the shop contained many artifacts, tourist trinkets and such. Many shelves covered all the walls along with a few counters spread out within the interior.

The antiques dealer released David from his warm embrace and nodded to the open door leading into the back of the musty shop. "This way. I have the document all prepared for you. You should have enough light."

He handed the seasoned archeologist a pair of white cotton gloves as they headed to the back. Ahmed put on white gloves as well.

Near the back of this private room stood an old wooden table with a light turned off just to the side. Two worn wooden chairs were positioned in front of the table. An ancient scroll lay there partially opened. An old wooden box and some plastic holders were beside it. Light shone in from a nearby window.

The scholar of history and archeology stepped forward, and bent down to examine the document. With his gloved hand, he gently unrolled the scroll like a child unwrapping a precious Christmas gift. A magnifying glass lay within arm's reach so he grabbed it and continued perusing the ancient scroll. The musty smell of leather, paper and other items assailed his nose. He always loved the smells associated with old libraries and research rooms. It gave David a feeling of comfort.

As he carefully scrutinized the scroll, a tingle of excitement ran up his spine. He could not believe what he was reading during his cursory glance. *Unbelievable*, he thought as he continued reading the Aramaic text. It was definitely late first or early second century script according to the style of writing. This was a scroll about Jesus as Ahmed had claimed earlier. This was amazing. What an incredible find.

He sat down on the old chair, took a deep breath and released it slowly. "How did you obtain this document, Ahmed?" he asked with excitement.

Ahmed sat down beside him and scratched his black beard. "The person I bought it from claims it was found near Mount Carmel in a small cave. He told me it was inside a clay like container with a top on it. The person that originally found it may have smuggled the document from Israel into Egypt many years ago. He kept it in a cool, dry place within his house. Eventually, he needed money and sold it to the fellow I later purchased it from," the antiques dealer's eyes gleamed with happiness as he narrated the events.

"Well, that makes it quite plausible as the ancient Essenes had an establishment on Mount Carmel with possibly a library there too. Aramaic would have been the language they spoke and wrote in. This may be a part of that collection that disappeared back then. It all seems to fit." He went back to reading the ancient Aramaic text mumbling to himself.

The scroll appeared to be written by someone who knew Jesus personally; the grandson of Matthew the tax collector. This was a totally new situation because all the four gospels within the bible and other biblical writings were written by others later on. None of these authors knew or had any association with the Master Jesus as far as anyone knew.

Finally, David sat up straight, rubbed his strained eyes and said, "Alright, I can buy this scroll from you, Ahmed, as long as we agree to our usual arrangement. In other words, once a museum, library or artifacts collector purchases the document, we will split the money down the middle."

"Agreed," Ahmed beamed and shook the archeologist's hand. "I will wrap it up for you in plastic and put it back into its wooden carrying case."

Both men had known each other for many years and were used to this mutually beneficial agreement.

After saying goodbye David took a taxi back to his rented apartment which was close by. He enjoyed watching the sights and sounds of this amazing city. This brought his mind back to the current world and relaxed him somewhat.

* * *

The archeologist cleared his head and came back to the present moment. The week had gone by very quickly for him. He'd been able to examine the whole document in detail and certain parts of the Aramaic text were ingrained in his brilliant mind. It was incredible that someone who had known Jesus had written these amazing words. The gospels of Mark, Matthew, Luke and John had all been written by unknown authors; who never knew this enlightened master. These gospels had been created supposedly after the death of Jesus the Master.

15

This document was unique, it was different. It contained messages from Jesus that were spoken to a living witness, Matthias the grandson of Matthew the tax collector.

David carefully and lovingly put the ancient scroll protected in plastic sheets into the old wooden box that was used to house it. He turned the light off, removed his white cotton gloves and stood up. He stretched, yawned and headed down the hall to his darkened bedroom. He undressed down to his underwear, climbed into bed and made himself comfortable. David was very tired.

He thought of all that the document would mean to our modern society and to various religions of the world. This ancient scroll would change history.

He shut his eyes and drifted off to sleep like a new born baby. He needed his rest because the next day he would tell the world his story.

Chapter Two
Alexandria, Circa 92 AD

Matthias sat quietly in a corner of the shaded courtyard and gazed at the people before him. They had all come to Alexandria to hear about Jesus. The small crowd ranged from ardent followers of the Jesus sect to the merely curious, with a few strict Jewish scholars thrown in for good measure.

The master had been dead for a year now and yet the rumors still persisted. False stories were being spread throughout the Roman world about Jesus.

It was Matthias' intention to set things right, to tell the truth. He pulled nervously at his brown beard with his right hand and continued to look about the courtyard at the throng gathered here. There were rich as well as poor people conversing together in small groups of three or four. The teachings of the Master brought many individuals with a common belief, and from all walks of life and countries to gather under one roof. At least, something positive had been achieved through it all. Perhaps, there was some hope, Matthias thought.

At that moment, a portly but pleasant looking man wearing expensive clothing approached him, "Matthias, everybody is here. I think it is time to speak." A splash of sunlight reflected off one of the man's many rings that adorned his moving hands.

"Uh...oh yes, of course, Jonas." Matthias looked into the blue eyes of his host, smiled and rose to his feet.

Jonas turned quickly to face the crowd. Sweat dripped from his bald head as he addressed them all, "Friends and followers of Jesus, I thank you all for coming to my house on this special occasion. The response to my announcement that Matthias, the grandson of Matthew the disciple, would be arriving here in Alexandria to speak to our organization is overwhelming. I know that some of you came from considerable distances to be here. However, I believe it well worth the journey. Come closer everyone and make yourselves comfortable as we listen to Matthias."

There were a few nervous coughs and some rustling noises as each person followed the advice of Jonas. Five young men who appeared to be friends sat down on the grassy area in front of the water fountain that was situated in the centre of the courtyard. Two distinguished looking older fellows sat down on the marble ledge of the fountain. Several wooden chairs placed about four cubits out from where Jonas and Matthias stood were filled quickly. Even a few women could be seen peering out from the colonnaded porticoes that surrounded three sides of the luxurious courtyard.

The grandson of Matthew, the tax collector, motioned slightly with his head and hands for the women to draw closer. Hesitantly, they joined the men. The two older men sitting by the fountain raised their collective eyebrows in a disapproving fashion but remained silent. Matthias could see the traces of smiles on the faces of the less rigid men, especially the young ones.

He took a deep breath in, released it and began speaking in his native Aramaic, "Friends, or perhaps, I should say brothers and sisters. There is a burning desire within me to speak to everyone I can about Jesus the Master."

Matthias then repeated his words in flawless Greek and decided to continue in this more universally accepted language, "The message I am about to pass on to you is profound and revealing. I ask that you all keep an open mind while I speak."

Amidst the small crowd, a dark haired man of middle years interrupted him, "Matthias, before you continue, I need to ask you a few pertinent questions. My name is Salinas. I am a trade merchant and have traveled about the Roman world. I have heard many astounding things about Jesus. From one side of the Great Sea to the other, I continue to hear similar stories about this man."

Salinas paused for a moment and looked about him with very dark intense eyes. He focused back on Matthias and asked, "Did he really rise from the dead after his crucifixion? Was he truly born of a virgin just like the Greek hero Hercules?" Even before Salinas had finished, many more started asking questions and making comments. Jonas hushed them all with frantic gestures.

"Be patient, everyone," Matthias said. He collected his thoughts and continued, "I wish not to offend anyone but there are some stories and rumours being told about Jesus in every city and village that I visit. The resurrection story has been with us from the very beginning. However, the second question that Salinas has raised is connected to a very recent rumour that has surfaced."

Cries of dismay arose. It was obvious to Matthias that many in the crowd believed all the tales that they had heard about the Master. The virginal birth concept, although recent, was gaining a foothold in the Jesus sect.

"Please, please. Let me continue. All your questions and concerns will be answered shortly as I relate to you the life of the Master."

The courtyard became as silent as an empty tomb. Eager faces looked at the tall, handsome man standing before them.

Matthias' voice took on a commanding quality, "This is the story of Jesus and what really happened."

Chapter Three
Jerusalem, Circa 2 BC

A bright light shone in the night time sky at the time Jesus was born. Astrologers in several lands including Egypt and Persia, gazed at this great event and believed it was a sign that foretold of the birth of a great human.

No one truly knew what caused this bright light or star to appear but many people could see it clearly. To all it meant something special was happening.

King Herod the Great was a ruthless and tyrannical ruler of Judea. He had murdered some of his family members as well as his wife, Mariamne. Many rabbis were killed by this man as well. Whenever he murdered someone, he would go into a depression followed by an ambitious building project. Due to the many murders, numerous building projects took place. He was considered mad by some and was paranoid. He guarded his own kingdom with a jealous zeal.

King Herod gazed out a window from his palace in Jerusalem. Both awe and fear gripped his heart as he looked at the light in the night sky. The light had become less pronounced the last few nights.

He turned quickly and looked at the guard standing nearby, "Fetch my philosopher, Samuel. I need to talk to him. Go quickly!"

Herod went back to staring out the window at the bright light in the night sky. He desperately needed to talk to Samuel. He wondered about the birth of a great person who would become a king. He had no intention of letting anyone become a king in his own country of Judea. Let it happen somewhere else.

The sound of several footsteps coming down the long hall drew Herod's attention back to the great audience chamber. As

he looked, two figures came through the opening and entered the large room.

The first man was short, bald and heavy set. A long grey beard covered his facial features. Sweat shone on his forehead. Samuel was still a pleasant looking man who smiled easily.

Just slightly behind him came Marcus Longinus, a Roman Centurion who was dressed smartly in his uniform. Marcus was a tall, handsome middle aged man who walked with a military bearing like he was on a parade ground. Both of the men entered the great chamber together.

Although Samuel had his ready-made smile on his lips, he glanced over at the Roman officer with a warning in his eyes. Marcus picked it up quickly, then looked forward towards King Herod. Yes, the mad gleam could be seen in Herod's eyes.

The Roman Centurion had noticed more of these mad glances in the last few years. He knew to be careful with what he said to Herod when these strange moods came upon him. The King of Judea had always been moody, unpredictable and prone to violence. Lately, the moods had become worse. An increasing paranoia was a part of this as well.

"You summoned me, your highness?" asked the philosopher as he nervously adjusted his expensive gold trimmed robe. Worry was on his bearded face.

"Yes. Yes. I need you to tell me again about the strange star in the night sky. The one that seems to shine upon Bethlehem. Is this the sign of a future great King of Judea being born now? Do I have to be worried? What should I do?" Herod fretted and bit his lip as he waited for answers to his questions.

"As I stated before, it is the sign of a great human being been born. Even the three wise men who came here last week said you have nothing to fear. They were on their way to worship him as a Messiah and great teacher. The ancient writings say he will be born in Judea in the village of Bethlehem. He will be great leader and teacher, and take our nation back to glory and greatness."

Samuel took a deep breath and then smiled showing his teeth, "But this event will not occur for many years. It does not affect you at all."

Herod paced back and forth throughout the huge chamber in a state of anxiety. He clenched and unclenched his fists. He grabbed a silver cup full of water and threw it against the wall.

The old philosopher continued nervously, "Your future heir will not have to worry as all these momentous events will flow in harmonious ways."

"And you, Centurion Marcus. What do you say to all this? Is there a threat to my security? Do I need to take any precautions?" Herod's eyebrows went up as he spoke Greek.

Marcus Longinus, a seasoned soldier charged with giving the King advice in regards to all matters of security thought carefully before he spoke, "No, your majesty, all is as it should be. You are secure in your esteemed position as the head of your country. I have been in constant communication with Emperor Augustus. You are still recognized as King of Judea with the approved backing of Rome."

Marcus hoped this answer would calm the fears of King Herod. But it only calmed the paranoid man slightly. The frantic pacing stopped.

King Herod rubbed his chin as he thought, "I know what I can do to ensure my kingship. I can have all the male children under the age of one killed. This will end the threat. If this great one is dead then the prediction will not come true. Yes, I will send my guards there tonight."

A wicked smile mixed with an evil look transformed the face of Herod. He now looked like a ravenous beast ready to pounce upon its helpless victims. "Centurion, you will lead my men to Bethlehem and direct them to kill all the male children under a year of age. Even if the boys are older kill them too."

Marcus usually kept his face calm and unreadable as he went through the business of the day. These words shook him to the core. He could not believe what he had just heard. Shock showed clearly on his handsome face.

"What! Are you serious? That would be horrible. As your adviser on security, I strongly disagree. The angry backlash from citizens would be great," protested the Centurion. He almost called Herod insane but caught himself. Of course, the king was insane and paranoid as well. That unspoken comment would probably cost Marcus his life if he had uttered it.

"I do not have enough soldiers here to protect you if the people rebelled," explained the Roman Centurion.

Herod let his mind drift for a moment. He imagined what the scene would be like in Bethlehem if he let his soldiers have free reign. He could see his men with blood dripping from their swords as they chased mother's holding their infant sons. Screaming and crying could be heard in the village. Herod envisioned a soldier plunging his sword into a small child and then wiping the blood from his sword off onto a cloth placed on a cheap wooden table.

Suddenly, he could hear some voices in the back of his mind saying, "King Herod, you need to focus. We need you here in the room."

"Wha...?" He looked around him, and saw the philosopher Samuel and Marcus, the centurion, staring at him with concern. The King was now fully concentrating on where he was. The violent scene had left his mind.

Samuel piped up at that point, "The peace would be shattered if you slaughtered those innocent children, your majesty. Remember what the Magi, the three wise men said about this special person?"

"Hmm. Yes, they all agreed that the great one being born would be a spiritual teacher and not a political power. They all believed he would not be King of Judea. That was a week ago," contemplated King Herod. He seemed a bit calmer as he spoke these words.

He now recalled that even the High Priests and Teachers of the Law confirmed the same prophesy.

Samuel glanced at Marcus quickly, relief on his face. It seemed they had calmed Herod the Great down. A dangerous event had been avoided.

Marcus cleared his throat and spoke in fluent Greek, "I must remind you that I am your adviser appointed by Emperor Augustus in Rome. Therefore, I take my orders from either the Emperor or in certain cases, the Governor in the province of Syria. With deep respect I say this Great One that I merely advise you. I do not take orders from you."

The Roman Centurion was now sweating profusely and was waiting nervously for the King's response. *By all the gods!*

thought Marcus, *I hope this crazy bastard does not kill me for that comment.*

It was rumoured that Marcus was in line to become a tribune once this difficult tour of duty was over. He came from a senatorial family and was qualified for this position. As far as he was concerned, he had earned the promotion a dozen times over.

A slight smile graced Herod's large face as he looked directly at the Roman officer with the close cropped hair who stood before him. "I know the arrangements, Centurion Longinus. Thank you for your sage advice. Is there anything else you wish to discuss with me?"

"I just wanted to let you know that the new guards have been fully trained and are posted with the rest of the contingent. Everything looks great. You are well protected, your majesty."

"Excellent. You are free to go, Centurion. Good night."

Marcus saluted him by putting his fisted arm onto his armored chest and then turned exiting the great audience chamber.

All the tension that had been there was now gone. Suddenly, Herod grabbed his oversized stomach and moaned. The nearly constant pain was back. For the last few years, he had suffered pain in his abdomen. In the last month, the episodes had increased in both severity and duration.

"Shall I call for your physician, your majesty?" asked Samuel looking concerned.

"No. No," gasped Herod still clutching his massive stomach. Wheezing from his asthma made it hard for him to talk properly. The recent excitement had set off this condition.

Herod pointed to a wooden table a few feet away where a bluish glass container sat. "My pain medicine is there. Bring it to me," he gasped a bit, took in a few breaths and then relaxed as the spasms ceased.

Samuel rushed over, picked up the medicine bottle and walked back to the king. Herod grabbed it, took out the stopper and hungrily guzzled the liquid that was within. He waited a moment and then drank a bit more.

The old philosopher thought his superior had taken too much pain medicine but kept quiet. At least, this would help ease the pain and let King Herod sleep. The bottle was put down on another wooden table nearby.

"Will that be all for tonight, your majesty?" asked Samuel as he smiled again.

The King of Judea nodded and then motioned with his hands for his servant to leave the great chamber.

As if by magic, two guards immediately appeared in the room and then followed their monarch as he walked into the bedroom chamber that adjoined the great room. Automatically, the men closed the doors giving the king privacy. Both men holding their spears took up their sentry duties opposite each other. This was a regular routine for them.

Herod crawled into his massive bed that was decorated with pillows and cushions like a wounded lion entering his lair. He closed his bleary eyes letting the medicine take effect. A warm pleasant feeling filled his head and eventually his whole body. The pain disappeared and he was about to drift off to a merciful sleep. The poppy seeds and other herbs were working their magic.

At that moment, a bright, almost blinding light appeared at the foot of his bed. Herod the Great opened his eyes and shaded them with one hand. As he looked, a large male angel dressed in a white robe and holding a golden sword stared back at him. The angel of the Lord spoke with a powerful voice, "Herod, I am the Archangel Michael. If you had tried to murder the innocent children in Bethlehem, I would have stopped it. I would have destroyed you and all your men. You have been warned. Know that you will remain King of Judea for the rest of your life. You have nothing to fear from this special child that has been born. Go to sleep and let things flow as they are planned."

Incredible energy radiated outwards toward King Herod and filled him with fear. He whimpered like a baby and then closed his sleepy eyes as the light in the room disappeared along with Archangel Michael.

Outside the bedroom chamber, both guards slept quietly as if in a drugged state. They were totally oblivious to the momentous event.

Soon, Herod dreamed of a time long ago when he was young, healthy and handsome. He was all powerful and ruled

Judea with an iron hand. He was loved by beautiful women. He saw many great buildings of stone surrounding him. Everywhere were these magnificent monuments that attested to his greatness. Herod would be King of Judea for a very long time. He entered a deep sleep letting this belief comfort him. Outside, the star in the night sky was still shining but less brightly.

* * *

The births had occurred over two weeks ago. Jesus was born first followed by his twin Judah Thomas a few moments later. Thomas was the Aramaic word for twin and this seemed appropriate. Joseph the father had picked their names quickly just after their births. Both baby boys were healthy.

Mary, their happy mother looked down at the newborns as they slept peacefully. The time had gone by quickly. She was glad that they had decided to visit Joseph's extended family in Bethlehem where his cousin, Ruth, a gifted midwife lived. This woman had made the birth of the twins feel safe and secure. Mary felt blessed that they were here.

She recalled the visit by the three Magi or Wise Men shortly after the birth of the boys. Balthazar, Melchior and Caspar were their names. Dark skinned Balthazar had arrived from Egypt about the same time as the other two wise men. He brought myrrh as a gift for Jesus and his brother. Caspar and Melchior had come from the land of the Persians, and were followers of the ancient religion of Zoroastrianism. Zoroaster had been a great spiritual teacher in Persia who left his mark on the world. Balthazar was also a follower of this religion.

Caspar had beautiful long black hair the color of a raven. Melchior had hair the color of silver. At night-time, the moon and the stars made it shine giving him a mystical quality. Caspar was medium skinned and very handsome. Both of them stood out with their attributes. They exhibited a commanding presence. Both of these men were skilled astrologers and astronomers like Balthazar. The sign of the star was a prophecy that had come true. They all knew this event would take place.

Balthazar, along with the two other magi, sat down in the living area in front of Joseph and Mary. The two boys were sleeping nearby. The Egyptian Balthazar glanced at the boys fondly and then said, "As astronomers and astrologers, we all knew that a bright light would appear in the night sky at a certain time. We have been waiting for it for years. This has now come true. It is a sign that a great person or great persons will be born on earth. We believe that your sons are in fact these great or special persons."

"The bright light in the night sky is actually a celestial event known as a conjunction of planets. The conjunction of the planets Jupiter and Venus have created this welcomed event. We left our homelands just before the bright light became evident in the evening sky. As we travelled here, the light became visible and grew in intensity. I watched as the light eventually stopped and seem to hang over Bethlehem. So did my learned friends, Melchior and Caspar. I came from Egypt while they came from the ancient land of Persia. The planets moved across the sky until they reached their position in the night sky overhead. We wanted both of you to know this. Some divine inner guidance brought myself, Caspar and Melchior here at the same time. A powerful energy guided our way here. We feel blessed that we have been able to meet your special children and leave them with these lovely gifts. We know that your sons will influence this world in the future in a very positive way."

Caspar and Melchior had brought frankincense and myrrh as gifts, respectively, for the children of Mary and Joseph. The Egyptian magi had brought gold as a gift.

Balthazar was a large, powerful man who smiled and laughed a lot. He let a great laugh out as he finished explaining everything to Mary and Joseph.

The three wise men or Magi then stood up, and nodded at the parents of Jesus and Judah. They left the large grotto being used as living quarters and returned to the inn nearby where they were staying.

* * *

One morning, the three wise men came into the huge grotto where Mary and Joseph were staying. Several areas had been turned into bedrooms. It was actually a home owned by fellow Essenes who were their friends.

Balthazar spoke on behalf of all of them, "Joseph and Mary, we must leave for our homes now. Last night all of us had the same prophetic dream. In it, we were warned by an angel to not return to Jerusalem and report to King Herod of our visit. The male angel warned us that our lives would be in danger if we did so. He might kill all of us." Balthazar took a deep breath, looked at his fellow astrologers and continued, "So, we will leave now for our own safety."

The other two Magi murmured their assent at these words of warning. Caspar and Melchior looked sad about having to leave but knew it was necessary. Tears filled Mary's eyes as she hugged all of them and kissed their cheeks. Joseph kept his composure and hugged them too. Both Mary and Joseph would miss the wisdom and love of these amazing astrologers.

That night, Joseph and Mary stood outside the village of Bethlehem, and gazed up at the evening sky. The star that had shone over this small village was almost gone. Joseph then looked over at his beautiful wife and said, "When we leave Bethlehem, we will head to Egypt and stay with fellow Essenes. We will remain there until it is safe to return home to Nazareth. We will let all our friends tell anyone who asks about us that we have left for Egypt. This should give us some protection from King Herod's men if we need it."

Mary agreed with a gentle nod of her head covered with radiant hair and looked up again at the many stars in the sky. She felt safe and believed that God and the angels would protect her young family.

* * *

Joseph, Mary and their two small children lived at an Essene community in Egypt for a few years. As a young family, they enjoyed the beautiful Nile River and all the food that was grown there. Joseph as a master carpenter repaired wooden furniture and even designed some furnishings for many of the Essenes. Occasionally, a rich merchant sought out Joseph for his woodworking skills and ordered a customized piece of furniture.

They lived in a small home with a vegetable garden in the back. Joseph and Mary loved to do gardening. Mary also grew some herbs and sold herbal remedies to some of the local people. The climate here was ideal and the garden was used all year round. Sometimes, Joseph and Mary would go out in a boat onto the Nile, and fish. They caught a lot of fish and even shared some of it with their Essene neighbours. Life was peaceful and easy here. Food was in abundance.

As a skilled herbalist, Mary even worked as a healer on occasion. She would use the healing energy of her hands on the injured and afflicted once in a while. Soon, her reputation as a healer and herbalist grew in the local community. She felt happy and complete knowing that she could help others.

One day, a messenger arrived from Judea with welcoming news. He went into the main square of the small town where they lived. This town was not too far from the ancient and revered healing temple of Heliopolis. The town known as Midal was located south of the Nile delta itself just where the river opened up. As the messenger stood against a white washed wall, people gathered in front of him. Once the crowd was large enough, he unrolled a scroll and began to read aloud. "Announcement. King Herod is dead. I repeat, King Herod is dead. Augustus Caesar in Rome has divided Herod's substantial kingdom up amongst three of his surviving sons. His son, Herod Archelaus, is now the ruler of Judea, while Herod Antipas is the ruler or tetrarch of Galilee and Perea. His other son, Phillip, is the Tetrarch of Gaulanitus, Batanea and Trachonitus. Caesar has followed the written will of Herod the Great in making his decision."

Just after King Herod died, a small rebellion rose up. The Romans were quick and squashed it. His sons may be the official rulers of these lands but the Roman military still controls everything.

Mary and Joseph holding the hands of their twins as they stood in the crowd, looked at each other and smiled. Joseph said with joy in his heart, "We can now return to our home in Nazareth. We will finish our duties here and then head back to Galilee where we can raise our family. Our future children will be born there." They hugged and kissed each other as Jesus and

Judah Thomas looked at both of their parents. Soon, they would all be home where it was now safe.

A week later, once everything had been finished in Egypt, the family left for the Galilee district. They travelled by donkey caravan with other travelers. It was much safer to travel in larger numbers as bandits still plagued the routes that led back to Judea. The long journey was uneventful. Eventually, they all arrived back home in the small village of Nazareth safe and sound. It was beautiful here in Galilee. They had returned to their own Garden of Eden.

Chapter Four

Jesus and Judah attended the School of the Philosophers at Mount Carmel until the ages of fourteen. This establishment was operated by a sect of the Essenes of which the boys along with their parents were also members. This sect had spread throughout the Galilee and even into Egypt. Many of the members wore white or light blue robes. Several of them served their respective communities as healers.

At the school, the boys had been taught fluent Aramaic and Greek. Some of the philosophy of the Greeks and astrology as practiced by the Persians had been a part of their education. Basic mathematics and others skills were also included in their studies. The teachings provided here would help them greatly when they ventured out into the world that was clearly Roman. Part of the philosophy or belief of the Essenes was to be kind to others and never intentionally hurt another human being. They were also taught to render aid and comfort to their fellow man. Many of the Essenes provided healing services to the needy and destitute, a service that the Romans did not provide nor believed in.

Along with their special education, some basic healing techniques were taught to both of them. As well, a detailed study of herbalism was included. Medicinal plants that grew here and in the Galilee were identified, and their healing properties discussed. In a year or two, Jesus and Judah would go to the healing center of Heliopolis in Egypt to fine tune their healing abilities, and finish their unique training.

On the day that Jesus and Judah graduated from the School of the Philosophers, their parents along with a few younger siblings came to Mount Carmel. The boys were the oldest at age fourteen, followed next by their brother James who was twelve. Simon was ten, almost eleven and their sister Mary had just turned nine years of age. The other two children, the youngest, Salome at age seven and Joseph age five were at home in Nazareth. Some distant relatives were looking after them while Mary and Joseph were visiting Mount Carmel. As Essenes, they treated each other as extended family members and even combined their finances when needed.

Both Jesus and Judah were excited about finishing school, and returning home to their beautiful Galilee. Of course, they were overjoyed when their parents showed up with some of their younger siblings. All the children greeted one another by hugging and kissing each other on the cheeks. At the age of fourteen, Jesus and Judah were now considered grown men in the eyes of the law.

Joseph smiled with pride and happiness at his brood of children. He was especially pleased that Jesus and Judah had graduated from the school here in Mount Carmel. He hoped some of his other offspring could attend classes here for a year or two in the near future. Of course, money and family duties might interfere with these plans. His beautiful wife Mary sat on a stone bench underneath a palm tree and watched her children re-acquainting themselves. She enjoyed the warm breeze that blew in from the Great Sea nearby. The smell of flowers, grass and water felt wonderful.

That evening after the graduation, all of them sat outside in a beautiful garden and talked about many things. They would stay the night and then head back home to Nazareth in the morning. Jesus sat on a rock looking up at the many stars. His mind started to drift back a year ago when his parents had taken him and Judah to the temple in Jerusalem. He led the memories flood his senses. The smells, the sounds and the different people that filled the streets of this city came to life again. The temple that was built by King Herod was magnificent with its stone work. He loved this type of architecture. It was the central focus of Jerusalem, its crowning achievement. The huge outdoor courtyard was surrounded on all sides by stone columns that created porticoes. Shade could be found here under the porticoes. It was here that he and his brother met with some priests and teachers of the temple. These learned men either sat on benches or stood as they discussed spiritual subjects.

Soon, Jesus and Judah joined in the interesting conversations. All of these men were impressed by the mystical knowledge expressed by these two brothers. All of them smiled as the boys talked about the human soul. These priests and teachers were all members of the great Sanhedrin Council which ruled the city and Judea. The council consisted of seventy-one men who met on a weekly basis here in a special area of the great temple called the Hall of the Hewn Stones. They were divided into two groups, the Sadducees and the Pharisees.

The Sadducees were wealthy aristocrats that held powerful positions. The Chief Priest and the high priests of the Sanhedrin were usually Sadducees. This sect was very accommodating to Rome and wanted to keep peace. They were very political and power driven. The Sadducees denied the existence of a spiritual world. They did not believe in angels or demons. Also, they did not believe in an afterlife. When a person died, so did the soul. The Sadducees were very strict and looked after their own interests instead of helping the people.

The Pharisees were often middle class businessmen in contact with the common man. For this reason, they were held in high esteem by the people. They believed in a spiritual world, including angels and demons. They believed in an afterlife and the resurrection of the dead. They also believed that God controlled all things yet decisions by individuals could contribute to the results. They were religious and not political. The Pharisees held the minority of positions such as regular priests. They held influence over the Sanhedrin because of their affinity to the common man.

A tall handsome man wearing rich clothing and sporting a radiant brown beard introduced himself to the twins, "I am Joseph of Arimathea. Along with being a Pharisee, I am a merchant and trader. I have travelled the Roman world and met many interesting people. I find you two boys fascinating. Your spiritual knowledge is quite impressive."

"Yes, my brother Jesus and I love talking about spirituality, especially the human soul," Judah answered and also introduced both of them to this important man. "We believe that the human soul is eternal, and returns over and over into a human body. The body may die but the soul lives on."

33

Jesus continued with this theme, "Our souls return to the heavenly fields after the body dies. The heavenly fields are filled with angels and spiritual beings. These fields are divided into many sections. Heaven is very beautiful and peaceful."

Joseph smiled and nodded his head in agreement. "All of my fellow teachers and council members hold the very same beliefs. We are very pleased to hear both of you talking so passionately. If you ever need anything, feel free to contact me at my home here in Jerusalem or my office. I am very well known."

Another member of the group here said, "We are very happy that you showed keen interest in the matters of the spirit. We enjoyed talking with you both."

At the end of this discussion as Jesus and Judah prepared to leave the great temple, both replied in unison, "Thank you for your kindness."

As they turned and walked away, Joseph of Arimathea was struck with how much the brothers looked alike. Only the colors of their eyes differed. Jesus had beautiful blue piercing eyes while Judah had attractive brown ones.

* * *

A voice calling his name a few times brought Jesus back to the present moment. His mother Mary was sitting across from him in the lush garden beckoning him back from his daydreaming. She smiled at her oldest son and said, "I see you have been daydreaming again. I believe it is a gift you have."

Her handsome young son returned her smile and replied in Aramaic, "Yes. I love to do this. Sometimes I receive important information or knowledge when I let my mind wander. I remembered our trip last year to Jerusalem where Judah and I met Joseph of Arimathea. I believe there was a special reason we met this powerful man. He will play an influential role in our lives in the future."

"You receive many visions and insight about the future. I am sure you are right about this Joseph of Arimathea. The future will unveil itself and his involvement in all of it," Mary answered and then gazed out at the evening scenery within this peaceful garden. Tomorrow, they would head home to their small village of Nazareth. She couldn't wait to be at home amongst all of the Essenes there. They had a large garden that needed tending as well.

Just then, a shooting star shot through the night sky above. Judah thought that this might be a good sign of things to come. That night, they all slept well in anticipation of going to their beloved home in the beautiful Galilee.

Chapter Five

Herod Antipater or Antipas was now the Tetrarch of Galilee and Perea. These two provinces were considered client states of Rome. Perea was situated south of Galilee on the eastern side of the Jordan River valley. The lush Galilee was next to the Sea of Galilee. Herod was adjusting to being named the ruler of these two provinces by Augustus Caesar. He would have preferred being a king and not a tetrarch. Hopefully, he would be able to accomplish this in the future.

Herod Antipas began many great building projects here in his kingdom. A major part of the construction took place in the town of Sepphoris. This Roman town was considered the capital of Galilee and a fair sized military headquarters existed here. Herod may have ruled this land but the Romans kept a watchful eye on it at all times.

Stone masons, carpenters and other qualified craftsmen were needed for this huge project that he had initiated. Many workers from the area flocked to Sepphoris in hopes of finding good paying jobs.

This busy town was only three miles away from Nazareth; an easy walk for any healthy individual. In fact, the family of Jesus could see Sepphoris from their own home.

Joseph, Jesus, Judah and James found work here as stone masons and carpenters. Their work schedules were quite flexible. Sometimes, all of them would work long hours for several weeks. At other times, only part-time hours were involved.

It was during the slower periods that they helped Mary and the rest of the family with duties at home. A large vegetable garden was located behind their spacious home in Nazareth. Fruit orchards and vineyards surrounded the area as well. As a large family, all of them worked together in harmony looking after the fruits and vegetables. Some of the produce was sold to neighbours and a few of the Roman soldiers stationed nearby in Sepphoris.

Along with this, Mary, her daughter and namesake Mary, and Jesus and Judah Thomas collected herbs in the area. They would then prepare herbal remedies which they administered to needy patients. Some of the herbs were sold to neighbours nearby. The other two children stayed near their home and helped with various chores there.

Joseph maintained his carpentry business at home on a casual basis. His expert skills were appreciated by many people in Nazareth, and nearby villages and towns including Sepphoris. Therefore, he worked solely at the massive construction site in the Roman town as a carpenter. James worked alongside him as a carpenter's assistant, both in Sepphoris and at home in Nazareth. Jesus and Judah were fascinated by architecture, and worked as stone masons at the site.

Mary and Joseph felt truly blessed. They were quite comfortable in life. Their many children were all healthy and happy. They were part of the large Essene community in the Galilee.

The family may have followed the religion of Judaism but all of them were true Essenes in nature. The beliefs, customs and rites of this sect were most important to them. About one hundred years before, the priests and the Sanhedrin council in Jerusalem had forced many of the Galileans to worship as Jews. Hence, Jewish synagogues existed in parts of the green Galilee landscape.

Mary's three older sons, Jesus, Judah and James had worked at the town of Sepphoris for several years now. They all enjoyed the hard work as it kept them fit and strong. They took great pleasure in helping to create a beautiful town in Galilee. It was an amazing place with the new Roman buildings being erected.

Some of the wealthier people had constructed small estates here. This manifested work for such tradesmen as carpenters, mural painters, tile setters and others. Joseph took immense pride in his workmanship and greatly appreciated the steady work offered to him by these prosperous residents. He built many wooden chairs and tables either here, or sometimes at his shop beside his home in Nazareth. Then, he would easily transport these items on a cart to the appropriate customers in Sepphoris.

Jesus and Judah were very experienced and highly skilled stone masons, and sculptors. Although they both enjoyed this type of work, it was not what they wanted to do for much longer. Both had a calling, a deep desire to be healers and spiritual teachers helping the many people that truly needed them.

Lately, this calling had become more intense within their hearts and souls. They both knew that they would follow what was in their hearts in the future. But for now, they were content in helping to build a wonderful new city.

The day started off cool. It was refreshing after the many hot days experienced here in Sepphoris. Jesus and his twin brother, Judah were working at the lower market building. It stood at the corner where Cardo Street and Decumanus Street intersected. The upper market, the only other one, was located on a hill.

Sepphoris had grown from a town into a bustling city full of wealthy Jews, Greeks and some Romans. Elaborate residences were being built here. Scaffolding covered one outer wall of the market building. The market was being expanded upon. Many ropes were attached to lifting cranes and other machinery. Both brothers could hear the steady stream of curses in Greek and Latin as several labourers hoisted a huge block of stone up the outer wall of the building. Men waited above.

Suddenly, a rope snapped in two followed by a thunderous crash. A blood curdling scream came forth a few seconds later. Everyone stopped what they were doing. Several men were running towards the melee. Jesus and Judah did as well.

Petronius, the Roman foreman overseeing this project stood with his hands on his hips yelling, "By the fires of Hades! Get some poles or anything you can. We need to lift the stone so we can free the trapped men."

As the two brothers gazed at the sight, they saw the huge block of stone lying on top of two men. Only the upper torso of one dark skinned man could be seen. The other lighter skinned one was mostly clear of the huge stone except for his left foot. He was still screaming, "I'm in pain. Please, someone help me."

Many labourers and tradesmen were running forward with poles and a few spears. They all worked together in unison as Petronius directed in Latin, "That's it, men. Put the poles under the front of the stone. Now lift. One, two, three."

Judah ran forward as the heavy block of stone lifted up a bit. He dragged the injured man out and glanced quickly over at the other victim. It was too late. He was dead. His eyes were closed and blood covered the tunic in the exposed upper torso.

Three Roman soldiers appeared along with Nicolaus, a Greek physician. He said to the soldiers, "Take this injured man to my medical office over there." His stubby finger pointed at the small white house nearby amongst some shade trees.

The injured man was placed on a rudimentary stretcher and carried by the soldiers. Jesus grabbed one of the handles and assisted them. The man was not screaming as loudly anymore. He moaned and cried a bit as he was transported to the medical office. Judah followed all of them into the small building, and watched as the man was quickly removed from the stretcher and placed onto a wooden examining table. The three Roman soldiers left, leaving Nicolaus, Jesus and Judah alone in the room. There was a small room directly behind this main room. Light shone in from the window above.

The middle aged Greek physician bent down to examine the wound. Unfortunately, the left foot was crushed beyond repair. He asked, "What is your name?"

Nicolaus' new patient whimpered, gasped for air and then answered, "My name is Levi."

"Well, Levi. I have some very bad news for you. We have to amputate your left foot. Otherwise gangrene will set in and you will die. I can make the procedure as painless as possible."

"No. No. Not my foot! How can I work with only one good foot?" he asked with tears in his eyes.

Nicolaus showed compassion in his brown eyes as he replied, "At least, you will live and probably have a very long life. I am sure you will be compensated by the local authorities here. This should help a bit." The Greek physician then looked at Judas and Jesus, and said, "I am glad it is you two that are here. We can use some of those herbs you brought me last week. I think one of these herbs can take the pain away and even put Levi to sleep. Am I correct?"

"Yes," answered Jesus. He turned and went into the smaller room, and picked up the special herbal remedy that was already prepared in a leather pouch.

Both Jesus and Judah had gathered several medicinal herbs in the area, and prepared them for the physician. Everybody knew that sooner or later, these medicines would be needed. It was always best to be prepared for situations like this. The two brothers had also studied human anatomy in Egypt for a year when they were younger. Their training at Heliopolis would come in handy through the years.

Jesus handed the pouch to Nicolaus who then put some red wine into a wooden cup and poured the herbal medicine in. He used his fingers to stir the concoction up. Once ready, he lifted the head of Levi from the table and said, "Drink it all down. Then relax and shut your eyes. The medicine will soon work, and you will feel no pain and become very drowsy. Just relax."

Levi laid his head back on the table and followed the Greek physician's instructions. Soon, his breathing became slower and a peaceful look composed his facial features.

"Alright. Let's begin. I want both of you to take these leather restraints and tie his arms down. Then tie both legs down just above the ankles." He stepped back, and let Jesus and Judah carry out the work.

Nicolaus went into the smaller room and returned with a leather bag. He pulled out a wooden container and opened it up. Inside were sharp knives and other medical instruments. He chose one of the knives and removed it from the container. The bag was tossed aside. With a keen and experienced eye, the physician placed the sharp blade of the knife just above where the leather strap attached to the crushed ankle. "Okay, boys. Better hold him down just in case he wakes up and fights." He looked at both of the brothers and then nodded.

It was obvious that Nicolaus had amputated many a limb in his years as a physician. He sliced through the skin, the bone and meat of the upper ankle in several seconds. The crushed foot fell off. Blood was oozing out of the wound now.

"We need to cauterize the wound right away." He glanced at Jesus and then nodded toward the lit torch near the doorway. Jesus immediately grabbed the torch and carefully put the flame to the bottom of the leg where the severed foot once was. With care, he cauterized the open wound. The bleeding stopped. All three of them could smell burning flesh and blood. It had a sickly sweet smell. Through it all, Levi merely moaned and cried out quietly in his drugged sleep. His head rolled back and forth slowly on the wooden table.

As the physician looked up at Jesus and his brother, he noticed a glow about each of their young heads. He had seen this a few times before under certain conditions and wondered about it. So he asked, "I see a bluish white light around both of your heads. What am I looking at?"

Both brothers glanced at each other with knowing smiles. Jesus decided to answer for both of them, "The light you see around our heads is known as an aura. It is the energy created by our bodies, the chemicals within and the sunlight above that creates this phenomenon. It is the same as a light that is seen around a candle. It shows that we are healthy and of a very spiritual nature."

"Ah. I see. That is quite fascinating. Thank you for explaining it to me. I have read about the human aura in some Greek literature before." He smiled at Jesus and Judah.

Nicolaus had his patient moved to a larger building that was being used as a hospital. There were about a dozen beds within. Levi was made comfortable here and was watched by staff as he slept.

The Greek physician thanked Jesus and Judah for their invaluable help. Both of the brothers returned to their work site at the lower market building. The body of the other accident victim had been removed. Someone had even sprinkled some sand and sawdust on the blood. It was hard to tell that a terrible accident had occurred here.

They both went back to work and became immersed in their duties. The clinks of chisels and hammers could be heard. A worker would curse once in a while. A few supply laden wagons pulled by strong horses went by. Soon, the sun could be seen starting to set. Everyone shut down work for the day.

Jesus, Judah, and James along with their father, Joseph headed home for Nazareth. All of them were looking forward to a lovely supper and a quiet evening at home. They all talked about the numerous accidents that had occurred at Sepphoris and the unfortunate loss of life. The toll was quite high over the last several years.

"Let's hope it does not happen again," said Joseph as he looked towards Nazareth and walked on the well-used path.

The crimson sun was almost set when they arrived at their beautiful home surrounded by olive trees, shade trees and shrubs. This was their sanctuary where their souls would be at peace.

Chapter Six

After several weeks of working at Sepphoris, all of the men decided to take a break. There were a lot of chores to be done by all family members. Joseph had some furniture to repair for some neighbours nearby. He needed to catch up on his carpentry business as it had been neglected while he worked in the new city. James would help him in his shop.

Jesus, Judah and their younger sister Mary were looking forward to collecting some herbs in the area. The medicinal supplies were getting low and this was the perfect time to stock the shelves with various herbal remedies. Joseph's wife Mary needed to do some weeding in the huge garden. Some fruits and vegetables needed gathering.

James was becoming an accomplished carpenter who loved to help his father in the workshop attached to the large home.

"Look at the top of this table," exclaimed Joseph as he sanded the top down. "It is much smoother now." He lovingly ran his hands over the grain.

James bent down and examined the wooden top. He nodded his head in agreement.

Just then, Joseph's wife Mary announced, "The meal is ready. Come on everyone. The food is laid out on the table out back."

After a morning of carpentry work, both of them were hungry. They walked out of the workshop together and passed underneath some large shade trees.

Suddenly, Joseph clutched his chest and moaned, "My chest and my arms hurt. It is heavy and hard to breath. I kept feeling pain down both arms but thought it would go away." He fell to his knees and his face looked white. He had a terrified look in his brown eyes.

"Father!" screamed James. "What is wrong? I will get some help." In a flash, he went running into the huge vegetable garden, and looked for Jesus and Judah. Both of his older brothers were standing under an ancient olive tree talking and laughing.

"Help! Help! Our father is in pain," James was out of breath as he ran up to them.

They all turned as one and ran towards the workshop. As they arrived between the house and the carpentry shop, they spotted their father lying on the ground face up.

Like frightened children, all of them gazed down at their stricken parent. Jesus knelt down and asked, "What is wrong, father?"

Joseph opened his eyes and said, "My chest hurts terribly. I can barely breathe."

Jesus and Judah exchanged knowing glances. They both had studied human anatomy in Heliopolis in Egypt. They knew instinctively that it was Joseph's heart. He had complained about indigestion for a few days but nobody thought it was serious. He was having a heart attack. Quickly, they lifted him up and carried him to the back of the home. Joseph was placed carefully onto a wooden lounge chair that was positioned under a lush shade tree.

Judah ran inside the home into the room where herbal remedies were stored. He found something for pain and breathing problems. In a moment, he had the medicine prepared and brought it back outside for his middle aged father. Jesus lifted his father's head up as Judah slowly poured the mixture into the mouth of the stricken man. Mary and the rest of the family gathered about their patriarch. Concern was readily apparent in all their eyes as they gazed at the ill Joseph. Everybody felt helpless.

His breathing became laboured. His eyes were closed as he tried to relax. The medicinal potion was starting to work. A gentle, warm breeze blew across all of their faces. The smell of flowers and herbs were in the air. It was beautiful here under the shade tree. Joseph opened his eyes and looked at his loving family. Finally, his gaze locked onto his beautiful wife Mary. "I wish I had more time. I feel like I am letting my family down."

"Husband, be at peace. You are in God's hands now." She gently stroked Joseph's face. Tears glistened in her lovely blue eyes.

Joseph shut his eyes again and mumbled, "My parents are smiling and waving at me. They are beckoning me to join them. I can see other departed loved ones. It looks so beautiful and peaceful where they are." A smile graced his wind and sun burnt face. His breathing became slower. "I love all of you."

Everybody expressed their love also for their beloved father. Young Mary, his daughter, cried, "Papa, I love you too. Please do not leave us."

He reached his hand out and grabbed his daughter's trembling hand. He squeezed it with the little strength he had left.

"Mary, you will have a long and happy life. You will become a beautiful woman like your mother. We all have a time to live and a time to die. There is a season for everything. It is my time. Enjoy your life, my daughter."

"James, you are becoming a fine carpenter. Look after the business and be there to help our neighbours. You can still work in Sepphoris as well." Joseph put his hand on his son's arm and smiled.

He then turned his gaze towards Jesus and Judah. "I am proud of you both. You will do amazing things. As the oldest, you must look after the family and protect them"

Joseph shut his eyes. His breathing became even slower. He said, "They are all waiting for me in heaven. All my departed relatives are there. I feel at peace. It is time. Oh, what a beautiful light." He let out a final breath and his body became still. A slight light of energy lifted from his now lifeless body. Mary, his beloved wife, laid her head on his chest and cried softly.

* * *

The funeral for Joseph of Nazareth was held three days later. Many people gathered at the local synagogue to say goodbye to a wonderful and loving man. He had been a loyal friend to many of the residents in the area. The rabbi performed a caring ceremony.

The body of Joseph had been prepared in the traditional ways of the Essenes. It had been washed, anointed with fragrant oils and wrapped in white linen.

Just prior to the funeral in Nazareth, several people came by to pay their respects and to see how the family was fairing. One of the visitors was a beautiful young woman from the fishing village of Magdala. She was known as Mary of Magdala or Mary Magdalene. She possessed gorgeous dark hair, medium coloured skin and the most exquisite brown eyes. Although Jesus and Judah were grieving, neither of them missed the qualities of this gentle beauty.

She introduced herself and then said, "Joseph built a beautiful dining table for my family a few years ago. I live with my aunt and uncle. We use the table quite often. I am truly sorry about his passing."

Mary, now a widow, thanked this lovely young lady and so did the rest of the family. Mary Magdalene along with a few others were offered refreshments as they gathered outside. She noticed some herbs growing in the garden and remarked about them, "I see some dill weed, garlic, caraway and poppy flowers. This is a wonderful garden, Mary."

The matriarch of the family enjoyed the interest shown by this woman from Magdala. "You are welcome to visit us anytime. Perhaps, we can talk about herbs and healing in the future."

Mary Magdalene nodded her head in a silent agreement.

The body of Joseph was taken to a burial cave that existed not too far from the village. His remains were placed inside this tomb and a large circular rock was rolled into place. All members of the local Essene group knew that the soul of Joseph did not reside here. His eternal soul had flown to heaven. This gave the grieving family some comfort. Some frankincense and myrrh were burned just outside the tomb, and a final prayer was said by all.

Chapter Seven

Mary Magdalene and her aunt Myra came to visit the family several weeks later. Mary's aunt made the perfect chaperone for a young, unattached woman. She was still strikingly beautiful at the age of almost fifty. It was obvious that Mary Magdalene had inherited her great looks from her late mother's side of the family.

The front of the expansive home in Nazareth was encompassed by a white stone wall. A wooden gate led into the front yard where many shade trees grew. It felt cool and pleasant here as the two women walked toward the front courtyard. The recently widowed Mary was standing in this small courtyard and went to greet them both. She opened her arms wide, and hugged Myra first and then Mary Magdalene, kissing them on the cheeks.

The mother of Jesus and Judah Thomas was genuinely happy to see them. She even smiled for the very first time since her beloved husband Joseph had passed away. "Let us go through the main house and take refreshments out back."

The inside of the house was spacious with several rooms off to both sides. This home had many bedrooms which were needed to accommodate this large family. A well-organized kitchen was near the back with double doors leading to the outside. These doors were already thrown open letting the gentle breeze waft through the house.

They all stepped into the huge backyard where many more shade trees stood. Off to the left, a modest orchard of olive trees grew. It was the month of Marcheshvan in Judea, which fell between the Roman months of October and November. The black olives were almost ready for harvesting.

Just where the shaded area ended, a substantial garden grew. Mary Magdalene remembered this spot fondly. Many herbs were growing closest to where the ladies stood. Fenugreek was one of the useful herbs found here. Vegetables and some fruit grew in the remainder of this vibrant garden. Beautiful flowers were planted in several beds everywhere. A gentle breeze blew the many coloured flowers in an easy and carefree manner. It was as if God himself had painted the breathtaking scene before them.

All of Mary's children spotted Mary Magdalene and her attractive aunt talking with their mother. They walked towards the ladies as one unit with Jesus in the lead. Judah and James followed closely behind their oldest sibling. Myra and her lovely niece were greeted in an enthusiastic manner. Hugs were exchanged and cheeks kissed.

Jesus, now in his early thirties, smiled generously showing off his beautiful white teeth. His piercing blue eyes twinkled with delight. This added greatly to his attractive features.

Mary Magdalene also known as Mary of Magdala returned the smile in kind. Her captivating eyes held a strange look as she focused her attention on Jesus for a brief second. She then glanced at Judah Thomas and the rest one by one.

The special look shared between Jesus and Mary Magdalene had not been missed by Judah. He was not happy about it. He had to keep control of his sometimes fiery temper as anger and a touch of jealousy crept into him.

Joseph's widow looked at everyone and said, "I think I will stay here in the shade with Myra and have a nice talk. Jesus, Judah, and even James, can show Mary all the herbs in the garden and in the surrounding area as well. There are lots of herbs everywhere." She motioned to some chairs nearby, waved the rest of them away and led Myra to the wooden chairs.

Mary Magdalene walked between Jesus and Judah as they wandered through the family garden. Mary and Jesus kept glancing at one another, laughing, and talking. His twin brother noticed the constant exchange and became very annoyed at it. A tinge of jealousy pulled at his heart. *If only Mary would look at me that way and talk with me,* he thought.

Meanwhile, James and the rest of the younger siblings drifted away leaving the three older people alone. Soon, Jesus, Mary and Judah left the family yard, and walked amongst the gently rolling hills covered with much vegetation. Wild flowers grew in abundance. The ground looked like a multi-coloured blanket with a green background.

"Ah. Those vibrant red flowers on the left are poppy flowers. We gather them for the opium within. They are wonderful for dealing with extreme pain. The Greek physician Nicolaus in Sepphoris buys the finished remedies from us. We supply many other important herbs as well," Jesus beamed as he said this.

A radiant smile spread across Mary's lovely face as she heard this. An angry scowl covered the face of Judah, the twin brother.

As the three of them kept walking, Jesus announced unexpectedly, "Judah is a wonderful cook. He often makes delicious meals for all of us."

His brother was surprised by this comment. Jesus was actually going to let him get a word in edgewise. He beamed as he spoke, "Yes. I love to cook. There are lots of herbs that we use for culinary purposes here and in our own garden. For instance," he pointed to the lush green plant growing on a small hill beside them. "That is basil, and it tastes great in chicken and other dishes."

The young lady from the fishing village of Magdala looked at him now with interest. "Usually, it is a woman's work to cook. It is great to know a man can do it too and enjoy it."

They both laughed. Jesus eventually joined in reluctantly.

After exploring the countryside, they sat down under a huge tree and relaxed. The banter was light and easy. Poor Judah felt like he was competing with his twin for Mary's attention. He was greatly enamored with this beautiful young woman. He knew Jesus was too.

As Essenes, all of them were interested in healing and helping their fellow man. The subject soon came up

Jesus raised his strong hands and remarked, "The hands have the power to heal. Along with the heat of the body, a special healing energy can be released from the hands and fingers. This unseen energy that comes from heaven above can speed up the healing within a person needing a treatment. The laying on of hands is a powerful tool to help others."

The conversation continued as all of them discussed this fascinating topic. Judah added, "A person that can truly heal others works with energy from God and the angels too. We all have the ability to heal others but certain individuals can perform miracles. It is these miracle workers that help humanity by allowing healing energy to come down from above."

They all agreed. Mary Magdalene was becoming attracted to Jesus and his strong aura that seemed to fill the space around them.

It was early evening when Jesus, his brother and Mary Magdalene returned to the family home in Nazareth.

Myra and her niece had left Magdala very early that day, and had arrived in Nazareth after nearly a full day of travel. So, they were very tired. Mary, Joseph's new widow, prepared a space for them in the home to sleep. There was lots of room in the family home. Oil lamps and some bedding were laid out for their honoured guests from Magdala. After an enjoyable evening supper filled with laughter, everyone retired for the night.

In the morning, another wonderful meal was prepared by Judah, his mother and his younger sister Mary. Olives, cheese, goat milk and honeyed bread were spread out on a large table in the dining area of the house.

Mary Magdalene sat on a bench with her lovely aunt on her right side and Jesus on her left. Everyone noticed that Mary and Jesus constantly looked, and smiled at one another. Every time he said something in a joking manner, she would laugh.

Judah did not think his brother was all that funny but kept his mouth shut. He was simmering inside.

Finally, Myra and Mary Magdalene packed up their meager belongings, and went out front. The family of Mary had brought a donkey outside loaded with a few bundles of herbs and other simple gifts. James checked the bundles, placed the belongings of the guest from Magdala onto the little donkey and tied everything down. "Everything looks secure. The water sacks are full too."

The ladies thanked him. It was agreed that Jesus and his twin brother would go to Magdala in a few days to reclaim their humble livestock. They even made arrangements to visit Mary, and her aunt and uncle in Magdala regularly.

* * *

Over the next six months, Jesus and Judah visited Mary Magdalene, and her uncle Ezra and aunt Myra in the prosperous village of Magdala. They took time off from the grain planting season to do so.

Mary, and her aunt and uncle also came to Nazareth a few times. The two families were becoming close.

It became obvious to Judah Thomas that his handsome brother and Mary Magdalene were in love. He, reluctantly, acknowledged that he had lost in this battle of the hearts. Instead of saying anything, he decided to accept his lot in life. Who knew? Perhaps, he would find true love too.

The month of Sivan brought the dry season. For the Roman masters, it was known as the month of May.

Jesus wrote his Ketubah, his marriage contract then. It was early evening, the weather was warmer. He sat at a table with writing utensils before him. His left hand lay on an open scroll that was blank. It was too stuffy indoors so this spot beneath the massive oak tree was more comfortable. It was a favourite area for the whole family, especially when the hotter season was upon them.

He waved towards Judah and his mother Mary as they were walking back from the garden. Young Mary, James and the other siblings could be seen behind a growth of trees to his right.

Jesus lit the oil lamp as the sun set over the horizon. It cast a wondrous glow over the lush landscape. The colours danced off the leaves of the trees and bushes as the gentle wind blew. God, the Creator, was an incredible artist. The view was breathtaking. He let his mind wander as he watched the beauty before him.

Mary and her son, Judah sat down at the well-used table across from him. Both of them looked at each other with curiosity in their eyes.

"What is it, my son?" asked Mary as she learned forward and scratched her left ear.

51

"I am writing the Ketubah, my marriage contract. I need some help from the both of you."

Mary smiled knowingly. Judah kept an impassive face.

"Since your beloved father is not here, I can help you." For a moment, sadness passed over her still lovely features.

"That would be wonderful. Judah, you can help too."

His brother glanced at him not knowing how he could help. For that matter, did he really want to help his twin?

"You will take a copy of the marriage contract to Ezra, Mary Magdalene's uncle in Magdala. Also, the bride price will be offered by you. You have my permission to negotiate if needed. We can adjust the papers accordingly." Jesus smiled at his twin brother fondly.

"Yes. Of course, I will do it. I feel like I am stepping into our late father's sandals. It will be an honour, brother." Judah Thomas was conflicted inside. He loved his brother dearly and would do just about anything for him. But his feelings for Mary Magdalene burned within his being. He knew in time that the desire within would disappear like a grain of sand on the wind.

An ancient Jewish custom would be followed for the betrothal and marriage rites. It was always the father of the son who handled a great deal of the contractual arrangements and even picked the prospective bride for his son in many cases. The son could suggest his preferred bride but the father made the final choice. Fathers in Judea held great influence in society.

It was decided that some of the marriage ceremony in the upcoming month would contain a touch of the Essene ways. Both parties would be dressed in light blue robes for the wedding ceremony. A rabbi would perform the rites and an elder of the Essene community would say a blessing too.

Jesus and his younger brother James built a bridal chamber beside the family home. It was completed in record time. Now the wedding date could be announced.

Judah Thomas was still angry and jealous towards his twin brother Jesus. He kicked the base of a big oak tree with his right sandaled foot during a minor temper tantrum and hurt his big toe.

Mary, his mother, with infinite patience, counseled him then. Mary laughed and admonished her son at the same time,

"You need to learn to control your temper, my son. If you do not, you could get yourself into a great deal of trouble. Remember my words."

* * *

The marriage took place at the synagogue in Nazareth. Many Essenes, family cousins and neighbours came to this happy event. After the prayers were said in the local synagogue, everyone went outside to a lovely garden area. The bride and groom stood under a marriage structure known as a Chuppa. Here, their vows were exchanged, and then both of them, Jesus and Mary, drank a cup of wine.

An old man that was a beloved elder of the Essene community spoke the blessing in a strong, firm voice, "God, the Creator, above blesses the both of you in your new life together. May much joy, and many blessings fill both your hearts and your souls. May God's wisdom guide you. Amen." Amen was repeated by all present.

Jesus with his pleasant voice gave a brief speech about eternal love. The words brought tears to his mother Mary's eyes.

Afterwards, the bride and groom went to their private bridal chamber. Under Jewish tradition, the couple would stay in here for seven days. It was decided by them to shorten the time to only three days. This followed more of the Essene customs.

Outside, all the celebrants drank lots of wine, ate some food and laughed. When the delicious wine ran out, more wine, mostly red, was brought in, literally, in a wagon hauled by two black horses.

Musicians hired by the family played a couple of flutes along with a lyre and a harp. One of them beat a drum slowly. Guests danced to the music and a few voices sang joyously. It was a wonderful celebration for all.

Within the bridal chamber, Jesus and his beautiful bride experienced each other intimately for the very first time. It was early evening, the sun had just set an hour earlier and was replaced by a half moon in the Judean night sky. It was warm and pleasant within the cozy chamber. A small window positioned high up on a wall let in some of the mystical moon light. A slight sheer curtain over this window along with some lighted candles created a magical ambience in here.

The gorgeous Mary Magdalene lay naked beneath Jesus. The light of the candles and the moon glistened off her lovely, brown skin. To Jesus, she was the most beautiful and exquisite woman he had ever seen. Her enchanting eyes smiled at him. "Come to me, my love," she whispered and raised her arms toward him. He bent down and kissed her passionately.

That night was the most magical night of their young lives. Love filled both their hearts. Intense joy filled their youthful bodies.

On the third day, they came outside the bridal chamber holding hands and smiled at all the waiting guests. Some of the people were still inebriated. A loud cheer went up. Jesus and Mary Magdalene were now married, and recognized as husband and wife.

Chapter Eight

Jesus and Judah Thomas kept hearing stories about John the Baptist, their first cousin. He baptized many people beside the Jordan River just south of the Galilee. He was an Essene but belonged to the strict order in Qumran by the Dead Sea. Many people including some of his devout followers claimed he lived in the wilderness, wore animal furs and ate locusts. He was considered to be a great orator and spiritual teacher. Both of the brothers felt that they were ready to start their ministry together and they wanted to be baptized by their famous cousin first.

The family was financially comfortable now and their younger brother James still worked as a carpenter in Sepphoris as well as maintaining a part-time business at home. So, Jesus and Judah decided it was time to follow their true callings since the family was looked after.

The two brothers along with Jesus's wife and constant companion, Mary, left Nazareth early in the morning. It was a full day's travel by foot to where John the Baptist baptized and preached to his numerous followers. The spot was near the Jordan River on the east side and about five miles north of the Dead Sea. Sandstone piers with steps led down into the water that was joined with the Jordan. John the Baptist had administered to his growing flock in this isolated place for many years now.

When the three of them arrived along with a supply laden donkey, they could see at least a hundred people standing by the site. A tall, well-built man with long brown hair and a bushy beard could be seen waist deep in the water just below the sandstone steps. A powerful voice boomed from this man dressed in animal furs, "Heaven is near. Be baptized and receive the blessings of God above. Rejoice. Be reborn."

A young woman wearing a white gown stood in front of him in the water and trembled slightly. John put one hand on her lower back and the other hand onto her forehead. He lowered her young body backwards into the water in a well-practiced motion. He held her head below the surface for a few seconds and then brought her back up into an upright position. Her black hair was soaked and she gasped in fresh air. "You are baptized in the name of the Holy Spirit. You have been reborn and cleansed of your sins. Rejoice and praise the Lord."

In unison, everyone yelled, 'praise the Lord' including the newly baptized follower. She started to cry with joy, and then slowly climbed out of the water and onto the sandstone steps. Her family members waited at the top of the steps beside a stone wall.

John the Baptist looked around at all the people who had come to hear him speak. A few white clouds floated lazily by. A warm breeze blew across his muscular form. The warmth of the sun felt wonderful on his wet body.

"You are all a part of the Creator. Your eternal souls are divine and connected to heaven above. You are God's chosen, God's children. Let the love in your hearts fill you with joy. Love your neighbours and friends as you love yourself. Do good deeds to others."

At that point, he glanced up the old steps and saw his cousins, Jesus and Judah standing there. Smiles graced their handsome faces.

John raised his powerful and tanned arms beckoning both the brothers to descend the steps, and join him in the water.

Everyone watched including Mary Magdalene as Jesus and Judah walked down the sandstone steps. The sun went behind a cloud and the scene became a bit darker. The twins stepped into the cool water up to their waists. John gave both of his relatives a powerful bear hug almost lifting each of them out of the water.

"It is great to see both of you," he said as he scratched his long, unkempt beard. "What brings you here? Are you both here for a visit?"

Judah answered, "We have come to be baptized by you, cousin. Then we can start our own ministry."

John looked at Judah Thomas in surprise and then Jesus. "I am not worthy to baptize you."

"You are worthy to baptize us, John," stated Jesus as he smiled pleasantly. "The Creator has given you the power to baptize his children. Are we not his children, also? It is part of God's plan."

"Fair enough. I will baptize you first, Jesus. Step forward."

Judah moved back out of the way as his brother followed John's command. The Baptist dipped his cousin into the water in the same manner as he had before. "I baptize you in the name of God and the Holy Spirit. You are reborn. Rejoice." Effortlessly, he brought Jesus back up into an upright position. The sun that had been hiding behind a large cloud appeared and shone down on Jesus. He raised his arms. His light blue coloured robe was drenched. The light from above shone directly onto his head and face. The brightness seemed to surround his whole being. The spectators gasped in awe at the incredible sight. They did not fully understand that Jesus had attained Cosmic Consciousness at this momentous moment. Divine energy from the heavens above had come down into his head and body. For one brief second, the Master Jesus had connected with the heavenly fields and been touched by the angels above. Some people would refer to this as being touched by God, the Creator.

Jesus put his arms down by his side and thanked his cousin. The sun now went behind another cloud. He stepped out of the water onto the sandstone steps and walked back up the slope to where Mary Magdalene waited under the slight shade of a palm tree.

It was now Judah's turn to be baptized. The tall, powerful cousin stepped forward a few steps and performed the same baptism ritual on Judah Thomas. When he brought his cousin back out of the water and into a standing position, Judah raised his arms upwards. The sun was still hidden behind a large cloud. No light came down around the twin brother of Jesus. Nothing miraculous occurred. John proclaimed similar words as before.

Judah thought, *It figures. Great things always happen to Jesus. I wish something wonderful would happen to me once in a while.* He had come to the conclusion that this was the way his life would always be. In any event, he was happy to have been baptized by his famous cousin John the Baptist. As a student of the mystery school, and healing centers in both, Heliopolis and Mount Carmel, Judah was fully aware of what had really transpired.

That night, the three of them stayed with John the Baptist as honoured guests. He had a small cave nearby where he slept and meditated. Jesus, Judah and Mary made two makeshift tents out of blankets, and some branches of wood. There were about another dozen people with beds made out of mats and blankets. They would sleep under the sky. This was a normal event outside John's sleeping quarters.

A roaring fire blazed not far from John the Baptist's humble cave. Everyone sat around it gazing into the mesmerizing flames. Andrew, a fisherman from the villages of Capernaum and Bethsaida on the Sea of Galilee was there. He had been a loyal disciple of the Baptist for two years now.

As the fire burned brightly in the night, all present were in a very relaxed state. Jesus cleared his throat, gazed at everyone around the fire and said, "When you are baptized with water, your true soul within is baptized in the name of God, the Creator. This ritual allows you to re-connect with heaven above. Sometimes, your spiritual and psychic abilities will be awakened after this special ceremony. Always remember that your human soul is eternal and a part of the Creator above. Know that on some level, you are divine within."

He had everyone's attention now. Andrew raised his arm like a small child in school and asked, "If our souls are truly eternal and connected to the Creator, will we return to heaven at the time of our physical deaths?"

"Ah. That is a very good question, Andrew. The answer is yes. You will surely see the splendours of the heavenly fields above when your soul departs this earth."

Another man with a balding head sitting beside Andrew leaned forward and asked Jesus, "If we are wicked and evil while we live on the earth, will we go to heaven or some type of hell? Jesus the teacher looked across the blazing fire at the man and responded, "There is no hell. If you are wicked and evil while on this earth, you will not be punished in that way. You will simply go to a special place up in the heavenly fields where an angel and perhaps, a departed loved one will counsel you. You can review that lifetime and know where you need to change your actions in the future. The angels and the spiritual beings in heaven do not judge us. So, do not judge yourself."

"What can we do to help while we are here on earth? Can we correct the problem?" a middle-aged woman who with a pretty face asked these questions.

"Forgiveness is the key. You must not be so hard on yourselves. Know that as a human being, you are not perfect and will make many mistakes. Learn from your earthly mistakes and again, forgive yourselves." Jesus put his arm around his beautiful wife and kissed her on the lips.

Mary Magdalene leaned against her husband and continued gazing at the fire. Everybody was getting tired now.

John the Baptist stood up, stretched and announced, "It is getting late. I think we should all retire for the evening." With that, he waved at all his guests in a carefree manner, turned and went into his small but cozy cave.

All the guests followed his example and went to their own sleeping spots. Judah Thomas crawled under the blankets underneath the makeshift tent awning and curled up. He was asleep in moments.

Jesus and Mary crawled into their own tents, pulled the blankets over their tired bodies, and soon were asleep as well. The fire died down and the numerous stars shined above in the Galilean sky. Another eventful day had come to a close.

A beautiful day dawned in the morning. The sun shone brightly and song birds could be heard in the trees beside the water.

Breakfast consisted of dried fish, fresh figs and flat bread. Everybody laughed and joked after the simple meal. Jesus and his twin packed up the blanket rolls, and pulled down the makeshift tents. Judah put everything safely onto the little donkey. They said goodbye to John the Baptist and embraced him warmly one last time. Nods and waves were exchanged between all as Jesus, Judah and Mary left for home.

John took Andrew aside, put a strong hand on his shoulder and said, "You are to follow Jesus and his brother. They will be your spiritual teachers and guides for now on. My time is coming to an end. Hurry and catch up with them."

"But, John, you are my teacher. I am your loyal disciple," interrupted Andrew as he glanced after the departing trio. He wondered why John had said his end was near.

"You were my disciple. You are now their disciple. Join them, and then go to Capernaum and Bethsaida to call more disciples to their new ministry. Your brother Simon and others can be persuaded to join this spiritual movement. Now. Go!"

Reluctantly, the fisherman from Capernaum gathered his meager belongings and put them over his right shoulder. He said farewell to John the Baptist with a heavy heart, and ran to catch up to Jesus, Mary and Judah.

"Wait up. I want to walk with you as you head to Nazareth. I can continue on to Capernaum nearby."

They all stopped, turned and looked at Andrew as he ran to join them. Sweat beaded his brow. He wiped it away with a sleeve of his tunic. "John the Baptist has insisted that I become a follower, a disciple. I know he is right. I know many men in Capernaum that would join you and follow you both on your mission."

Jesus smiled at him in a knowing way. "We will return to Nazareth and let you carry on to your own home. In three days, we will journey to Capernaum to meet potential disciples."

Judah patted Andrew on the back in a comforting way. "We are honoured that you are joining us. If I remember correctly, your name is Andrew?"

"Yes. I have a brother Simon in Capernaum and my father Jonas. Both are fishermen in the Sea of Galilee. I am anxious to introduce them to you."

Later that afternoon, Jesus, Judah and Mary Magdalene took the road to the left that headed to Nazareth. Andrew kept on the main road which took him to the fishing village of Capernaum. The fisherman was tired but excited. He knew something great was about to happen. He could barely wait the three days until they all met again; this time in Capernaum.

Chapter Nine

The fishing town of Capernaum had about 1500 residents. It contained a synagogue as well as a small Roman garrison. It was a prosperous community. A farmers market was located at the edge of the town by the water. It operated every weekend. All the farmers and fishermen in the area brought their products here to sell. Many fruits and vegetables were available at this busy market. Even the Roman soldiers bought food products here.

Jesus and Mary Magdalene holding hands left the main road, and slowly walked the streets of Capernaum. The synagogue could be seen directly in front of them. This structure and the Roman garrison were the two largest buildings in the town.

Judah Thomas followed behind them looking at everything and everyone. Jesus and Mary entered the market area. Judah joined them a few moments later. All sorts of produce and fish were available to purchase. The newlyweds wandered from stall to stall and took their time. Judah enjoyed observing everything. They could see wharves and some fishing boats down by the water's edge as they moved through the market. Andrew was there beside another man helping with a fishing net.

Jesus led the way and headed towards Andrew the fisherman. He spotted all three of them, smiled and waved. He looked happy to see them. The man beside him was of above average height and very well built. He looked more like a Greek wrestler than a local fisherman.

As Jesus, Mary and Judah approached, Andrew introduced them to his stockier brother, "Hello, my friends. This is Simon, my older brother."

Simon carefully looked at each of them sizing them up. He said, "Hello. I am glad you came to Capernaum. My brother speaks quite highly of all of you. Unfortunately, you have come at a bad time for us."

Judah flicked his long hair back and asked, "What is wrong? Why is it a bad time?"

"For the last three days, my brother and I have caught very few fish. Some of the other fishermen have had the same problem. Our father Jonas became frustrated and returned home. I am as equally frustrated by it."

That is when Jesus stepped forward and said, "Simon, why don't we go out into the sea and catch some fish?"

"What! We have been out there since early this morning. We barely caught enough fish to feed our own families let alone feed others. Why should I waste my time?"

With a piercing gaze, Jesus replied, "Simon, let us go out together and cast our net. Allow me to pick the place to cast the fishing net." He walked up to the fishing boat that was beached on the shore and started to push it into the water.

With reluctance, Simon joined him and pushed the boat out. Judah and Andrew jumped into the boat with Jesus and Simon. They used the wooden oars and headed out into the Sea of Galilee. Mary Magdalene stayed on shore under a palm tree and sat down to relax.

Jesus scanned the horizon and pointed north. "Take the boat to that area, Simon." The small sail was set and then the wind caught it. The fishing vessel moved steadily out into the Sea of Galilee in a northern direction and the distant shore could be seen. It was a beautiful day out on the water. The sun warmed their faces and a steady breeze blew the smells of the water to all of them. Birds could be seen flying overhead. Several of the birds seemed to congregate ahead over top and some were floating on the water just below.

"That is the spot there," Jesus pointed again. He took in a deep breath and enjoyed the smell that assailed his nostrils. "Now. Stop here. Take the sail down. Andrew, toss in the anchor. This is the spot."

He grabbed some of the fishing net, and Simon and Judah followed his example. They cast the net into the calm waters and waited. Jesus and Andrew started talking about the mission that the twin brothers had just begun.

Andrew nodded at his brother Simon and exclaimed, "I have talked about joining your ministry as a disciple. I have asked Simon to join us on our spiritual journey. He is not yet convinced."

Simon glanced at his thinner brother and said, "If we can catch a lot of fish today then I will follow you both. I would consider it a small miracle if you can choose this fishing spot well." He laughed in a cynical way.

"Let us haul the net back up, everybody. I think it is time." Jesus started to pull on the net and the others did the same.

As the net came up, it was full of fish. The fish filled the inside of the fishing boat as they finished hauling in the net. Simon could not believe his eyes. He had never caught this much fish at one time. Yes, it was a small miracle.

"Well. I am convinced, Jesus. I will follow you and your brother as a disciple. I still need to be a fisherman part-time."

"Of course. You are a fisherman now. But I will make you a fisher of men."

Everybody laughed at this comment. Simon and Andrew were ecstatic at the fine catch. The sale of the fish would fill their nearly empty coffers.

That evening at the humble home of Simon, everybody enjoyed a fine meal. Fish roasted over a spit and seasoned with some tasty herbs was the main course. Cooked onions and other vegetables accompanied the fish. Figs, honey and some flat bread finished off the feast. Fine red wine flourished during and after the splendid meal.

Afterwards, the family along with Jesus, Judah and Mary left the front gates of Simon's home. They walked down to the water's edge where someone had prepared a roaring fire. All gathered about the blaze and made themselves comfortable. The fire crackled and sent sparks into the night sky. It was a warm, gentle evening. The stars were appearing slowly one by one.

Full stomachs, and warm glows from the wine put everyone into relaxed and peaceful moods. The night was becoming magical. Gentle waves washed upon the shore creating a fine effect. A slight breeze blew through the trees overhead.

Jesus sat beside Mary, grabbed a piece of firewood, tossed it into the blazing flames and looked at everyone gathered here tonight. Judah, his handsome twin sat beside him on his right.

Jesus then spoke, "As humans, we have many psychic abilities. We have these gifts buried within. With training, we can release these abilities. One of them is intuition, an inner knowing. This is a powerful ability lying dormant in all of us."

He sat back, reflected on his thoughts and then continued in a smooth, mesmerizing voice, "My brother and I were trained in Heliopolis in Egypt to awaken these dormant gifts. By relaxing and focusing on something you want, you can release the power of intuition. I used this power today in order for Simon to find and catch fish."

Jesus waited a moment to create the right effect and then said, "I prayed silently for the angels and heaven to help. Then I focused on the Sea of Galilee and asked where the fish could be found. In a few seconds, I was shown a vision in my mind where fish were a plenty. Of course, the hunch or intuition was right. We were able to catch many fish."

Simon and his brother smiled across the fire at Jesus, their spiritual teacher. Murmurs of appreciation could be heard within the group.

"My brother Judah and I will teach you these techniques. With practice, you will all become very good at following your intuition."

Simon scratched his reddish-brown beard and said, "I look forward to learning this and anything else from you. I suspect you have much to teach us."

"Yes," confirmed Jesus. "We will teach you many techniques. Mary, my wife will help you with healing techniques and the use of herbal remedies. It is our purpose to help others and relieve the suffering of the needy."

Quiet banter continued about the fire for a bit longer. The flames started to die. Soon, by ones and twos, people left and headed home to their beds.

The wife of Simon prepared sleeping mats in the outer courtyard for Jesus, Mary and Judah. The lamps were extinguished and soon the world was quiet. The stars shone above and a half moon filled the sky.

It was overcast the next morning and a bit cooler. After a simple meal, Jesus and Judah offered to help Simon and Andrew fish once more.

The sky was starting to look a bit threatening as the four of them left the shoreline behind them. The waves on the Sea of Galilee were starting to rise. They pulled on the wooden oars and headed deeper into the sea. Andrew kept glancing at the dark storm clouds overhead. He was starting to get worried.

In no time at all, the fishing boat was in the middle of the Sea of Galilee. As a team, all of them cast the net into the water that was becoming more turbulent. As they sat there, it started to rain lightly. It was unusual for rain at this time of the year but not unknown to happen on occasion. The wind picked up and the waves of the sea became higher.

Everybody looked at each other, and decided it was time to bring in the fishing net and head back to the safety of the shore at Capernaum. A small catch of fish was in the net when they brought it up. It was a small but adequate haul. The fish flopped on the bottom of the boat as they headed for shore.

The rain became stronger and the clouds darker as they made their way back. Andrew was very agitated as he watched the sea and the violent sky. Simon, his brother was nervous but appeared calmer. Jesus and Judah sat down on the benches in the fishing vessel, shut their eyes, and seemed to pray silently. Every once in a while, they would open their eyes and glance at the angry sky above. In a few minutes, the rain stopped, the blowing wind turned to a gentle breeze and the clouds became lighter. Soon, a hint of sunlight peeked out from the storm clouds. Even the waves settled down. The twins opened their eyes again at the same time, glanced around them and smiled. Everything was calming down.

Both Simon and Andrew looked at them in amazement. They wondered what Jesus and Judah had done. Did they actually calm the waves and the upcoming storm?

Judah Thomas stared at Simon and then Andrew. He smiled and said, "Sometimes if you focus and ask the angels to help, they will intercede and calm the weather. My brother and I visualized or imagined the weather becoming nicer. As you can see it worked."

Jesus nodded his head and added, "This is another technique we will teach you and other disciples that join our movement." He leaned back, took in a deep breath and felt the gentle breeze on his bearded face.

Simon the fisherman thought he should mention something. "There are a few others here, and in Bethsaida that want to meet both of you and follow you as disciples."

It seemed the spiritual movement was growing quickly. Jesus and Judah were happy the way things were turning out. Both of them looked at each other and came to the very same conclusion. They would live and work in Capernaum. It would be their home base to travel to and from. There were lots of towns and villages nearby that they would visit.

Once they came ashore, the small catch of fish was sold to many residents along with one fish merchant. The merchant had several customers in the area including a few Roman soldiers. He would quickly sell his share of the catch to these people.

Jesus and Judah announced to Simon and his brother in excited voices, "We have decided to stay in Capernaum. It will be our home base where we can travel out to other communities. We will preach our message and teach our lessons to the many who will listen."

Simon scratched his beard, glanced at Andrew and said, "The home next door to mine is vacant. I own it. You can live there as long as you wish. This is all very exciting."

Andrew added, "Matthew the tax collector lives here in Capernaum and John the fisherman lives in nearby Bethsaida. Both of them want to meet you tomorrow. I know many more will follow their example."

"We are looking forward to meeting them tomorrow. This is great," Jesus beamed with joy.

Judah continued, "Thank you, Simon, for your generous offer. We will be pleased to stay in the vacant home. There are so many places to visit and people to meet. We are truly blessed."

Capernaum was a wonderful town close in proximity to many towns and villages in the lovely Galilee. The twin brothers knew great memories would be made here. God's plan for them was unfolding here on the shores of the Sea of Galilee.

Chapter Ten

Herodias, with her hands on her shapely hips, glared at Herod Antipas, her husband. "I want John the Baptist arrested and executed," she spoke in Latin as she had been educated in Rome along with Herod.

"Why?" asked Herod as he stared at her across the large room. "He cannot harm us. He just talks and preaches a lot."

"He called me a whore when we went by him after leaving Tiberias. He needs to be punished."

"If I arrest him, many of his followers will be up in arms. I do not think it is a wise course of action, my love," soothed Antipas.

"He made a fool of me when we passed him by the river. Even the patrol of Roman soldiers thought that it was funny. I watched some of them laughing at me. I will not tolerate this type of treatment from anyone. Arrest that bastard now," Herodias shouted at him.

"Alright. Alright. I will send the captain of the guards with a small patrol to arrest him. Perhaps, a few months in a prison cell here at Machaerus will quiet his mouth. He is considered a prophet and his followers listen to his every words. We have to be careful."

"Who rules here? You or that locust eating madman. You are afraid of him," Herodias shrieked.

"Yes. I know he is a prophet with power over the masses. He could raise an army against me and start a rebellion."

"Then, my husband, stop him now. Eliminate the threat from this madman."

"Captain. Captain of the guards," yelled Herod as he went to the open door and glanced down the hallway of the luxurious palace. In a matter of moments, Jonathan, the captain of the guards walked quickly down the hallway, and entered the private chamber of Herod and his second wife, Herodias.

"Yes, your majesty. You called?" asked Jonathan, a rough and grizzled looking man with greying hair, and a slight belly. He spoke in Aramaic, the common language of the people.

"Take some of your best men and arrest John the Baptist. Bring him here and throw him in a cell in the lower city, far enough away so we cannot hear him."

"Yes. Tetrarch. It will be done." He saluted in the Roman way putting his closed fist over his armored and massive chest. He turned smartly and headed down the long hallway shouting orders for several men to join him.

* * *

John the Baptist covered his eyes with one powerful hand and glanced at the scenery around him. It was another warm day. With the sky overcast, the temperature was slightly cooler. This was a blessing to all assembled at the baptism site.

Birds sang in the background. Numerous species of birds migrated across these lands heading to Africa in cooler months and then north as the seasons warmed. It was a marvelous sound for everybody to hear.

A slight breeze blew across the bearded face of John. His hair was wild and stood out everywhere. He looked almost like a lion with a hairy mane. This created the impression of an intimidating beast standing at the foot of the ancient steps. Animal furs covered the torso of his muscular body.

"Friends. Who will be next to be baptized with water and receive the Holy Spirit?"

"John. John. Soldiers on horseback are approaching. There must be eight to ten of them heading for us. It's Herod's men. Run, hide!" a tall, thin man announced as he pointed south towards the patrol of Herod's guards.

"No. I will not run nor will I hide like a frightened animal. I will meet them proudly and without fear. I knew this day would come." John the Baptist stepped down into the cool water and waited his fate calmly.

He could hear the approaching horses and saw the dust rise. The patrol stopped just above the sandstone steps. A man at the head of the patrol yelled orders for all his men to dismount. Jonathan wearing brown leather and a brown helmet nodded at four of his soldiers to follow him down the steps.

"John the Baptist. You are under arrest as per the orders of Herod Antipater. You will come with us to Machaerus."

John stepped back further into the water and steadied himself.

The captain of the guard along with four guards went into the water and cautiously closed in on the Baptist. Hands reached out for the strong, tall man.

"I will not go willingly. I am God's messenger," he proclaimed, and grabbed Jonathan by his head and shoulders. In one smooth motion, John thrust the captain of the guard underneath the water and shouted at the sky, "I baptize you in the name of the Creator."

Jonathan broke free from the powerful grasp and came to the surface gasping for air. He pulled the long hair out of his face and reached for John the Baptist.

John put up an incredible fight. Effortlessly, he tossed two of the guards into the water. One of the other soldiers leapt onto his large back and wrapped his arms around him. Another one grabbed his right hand and pulled it back. It took several moments before they had the big man contained. A rope was tied tightly around his wrists. Another rope was strung about his waists.

They dragged him up the white steps to where the other guards waited. Many of John's followers were yelling and screaming obscenities at Herod Antipater's men. Accusations of, "Shame on you. He is a great prophet. Let him go," escaped many lips.

Several of the Baptist's followers ran towards the soldiers. The armed men drew their swords and readied themselves.

Seeing all of this, John yelled, "No. Step back now. Stay back from the soldiers or else they will kill you. Do as I say, my friends."

Reluctantly, the men along with a few women stopped and moved back from the armed patrol.

"Pray for me, people. Ask for God's deliverance." John the Baptist was now attached by his waist to a rope that hung tied to a saddle. His hands were bound in front of him. He was pulled slowly along while two mounted guards rode behind him.

The people shocked and angered still shouted threats and names after Herod Antipas's men, "Bastards. Go to Hades."

* * *

Later that night, John was thrown into a filthy cell in the lower city just below the opulent palace of Machaerus. Through the cell bars, he could see a window high up on the far wall. Some night light came through it.

Jonathan, the captain of the guards inspected his prisoner from the other side of the cell and said, "Do not bother to shout. They cannot hear you in the palace. Only a few of the workers in this part of the lower town would barely hear your voice. So, relax and make the best of your new living quarters." He laughed at his own words.

Herod and Herodias sat in their beautiful garden, and contemplated their earlier actions. The Tetrarch of Galilee and Perea believed everything would calm down, and then he could release the Baptist in a few months.

His beautiful wife sat on a comfortable divan and schemed. She would find a way to have John executed. She knew her husband did not want to kill the Baptist for fear of reprisals. She believed an opportunity would present itself to dispose of this locust eating preacher. She would strike when the time was right.

Machaerus, originally, had been a fortress built by the Hasmoneans. Herod the Great had done major improvements to the place turning it into a luxurious palace. He had installed thermal baths, a triclinium or dining room, and a magnificent garden filled with flowers and trees.

Herod Antipas or Antipater was a tetrarch or sub-king who ruled the provinces of Galilee and Perea. He may not have been a full king but he lived like one.

He and his scheming wife gazed out at the evening sky. The Dead Sea held a lonely yet beautiful view. They drank their quality red wine slowly as darkness filled the palace. Servants lit numerous oil lamps to dispel it. Another day had come to an end.

Chapter Eleven

The healing abilities of Jesus and his twin Judah Thomas were becoming known far and wide. Many people with afflictions would travel to Capernaum in the hopes of being healed by the brothers.

Their growing reputations had also drawn many new disciples to them. There were now twelve disciples in the inner circle plus Mary Magdalene. The brothers, John and James, fishermen in the Sea of Galilee, had come from the nearby village of Bethsaida to join the movement. Shortly after their arrival, Judas Iscariot sought Jesus and Judah out in Capernaum. He was included in the inner circle and was the treasurer of the group. Others, both men and women, were joining the fast growing movement.

Jesus would, occasionally, take a break from everyone and go for a walk by himself. The time spent alone allowed him to clear his thoughts and to make plans. He really enjoyed these rare moments. This would become a regular regimen for him in the near future.

As he was walking along the streets of Capernaum alone, a Roman centurion hurried up to him. "Jesus. I need your help desperately," he said in Latin and then switched to Greek. "My boy servant is ill and very close to death."

Jesus looked into the pleading man's eyes and asked, "Would you like me to come to your home to lay my hands on him?"

"No. I am not worthy to have you under my roof. Your presence is not necessary. I am a man of authority with many men under my command. When I say to someone, 'Go', they do as I say. When I say, 'Come', they will follow me. When I ask for something to be done, it is done. I know that you can heal my servant at a distance. I know it will be done. I have faith."

Jesus was astounded. He had never met anyone with so much faith. Even his own disciples did not have that amount of faith.

"Centurion. You show great faith. I am greatly impressed. Go and it will be done just as you believe."

The Roman centurion bowed his greying head humbly and then went home directly. He knew his boy servant would be healed.

If only more people would have the same amount of faith as the Roman centurion, thought Jesus as he kept walking. He spoke under his breath, "I will discuss this with everyone in the next few days."

The very next day, the Master Teacher went for another walk alone. He decided to leave the town and take a leisurely stroll in the surrounding country. It was beautiful here. The wildflowers grew in abundance.

Suddenly, a leper approached him from behind a large oak tree. "Master Jesus. Please heal me. I know you can." His disfigured face was covered by a dirty linen cloth. His hands were wrapped in the same material.

The appearance of the leper startled Jesus a bit. He gathered his thoughts and spoke in his native Aramaic, "I will lay my hands upon your head. God and the healing angels will heal you. I am merely a humble servant who directs the healing energy from the Creator through you." He laid his strong hands upon the afflicted man atop the head as promised.

Instantly, a great light came down from heaven above and poured through the top of the leper's head. Vibrant colours of white, blue, green and purple shot through the top, surrounded his whole body, and went deep inside the man. He moaned and dropped to his knees. Sobbing sounds exploded from his mangled lips.

"Something is happening. I feel warmth and tingling sensations everywhere. My face, my hands and my body feel different." He looked down at his covered hands, unwrapped the filthy cloth and gasped in amazement, "My hands are healed. It is a miracle."

Jesus spoke with authority, "Rise, my friend. You are healed. Praise the Lord and keep his commandments. Worship him in your heart and be kind to others. Do not tell anyone that I have healed you. Let this moment be between us."

The leper stood up and unwrapped the cloth covering his face. He felt his healed face with his now healthy hands. The healing light disappeared as if someone had blown it out like a candle. "I will worship the Creator in my heart. Thank you, Jesus."

He turned and ran through the meadows with pure joy within. Unfortunately, the former leper could not contain his excitement. He told everyone he saw of the amazing event. This story spread like wildfire through Galilee and even further abroad, even into Jerusalem.

Soon, Jesus along with his twin brother would be mobbed by the crowds wherever they went. Everyone wanted to be healed by them, especially by Jesus. It did not matter what the affliction was, people wanted to be healed by these miracle workers.

In the future, they would have to find a lonely, private place outside of a community when they went there. Otherwise, the people would gather in great crowds and press them for healing services.

* * *

Jesus, Judah, Mary and the twelve members of the inner circle sat in the shade by the beach at the Sea of Galilee. It was late in the afternoon. The waves splashed softly upon the shore. Capernaum was located at the northwest part of the sea. The fishing town of Bethsaida could be made out just slightly north and across from where they were.

Along with the twelve disciples, several women were seated here. These women were also disciples or followers of Jesus and to a lesser extent, his brother Judah. Judah had become a loyal assistant.

"Friends, my brothers and sisters, I wish to discuss a special healing method with you. A few days ago, a Roman centurion stationed here at the local garrison came to me and asked me to heal his boy servant at a distance. He possessed great faith and knew that the young servant would be healed in this manner. This method is called 'Absent Healing'. Both Judah and I studied this ancient healing technique while in Heliopolis. We will both teach this wonderful healing method to all of you."

He glanced at his twin who nodded in agreement. "We will be teaching this technique for the next few days. You can practice sending healing energy and thoughts to others at a distance. You should all be pleasantly surprised. The more you practice, the stronger the results. Always ask your healing angels to help too."

Everybody was happy at this announcement. Smiles and happy glances spread through the intimate group.

For the next few days, the disciples, both male and female, studied and practiced 'Absent Healing'. Many of them sent healing energy and thoughts of love to sick relatives who lived in other communities outside of Capernaum. Shortly afterwards, some of the disciples received encouraging written messages or oral ones attesting to the power of 'Absent Healing'.

It was now time to travel to the local towns and villages that were within a comfortable walking distance to Capernaum. The first place would be nearby Bethsaida. There was a large following there and many of the disciples knew people in this place.

Chapter Twelve

The small fishing village of Bethsaida was only a short distance from Capernaum, about four miles away. It was located where the northern shore of the Sea of Galilee and the Jordan River meet, and was part of the province of Gaulanitis. The town was positioned on the right side of the river on a hilltop that overlooked the sea. Fishing boats were beached or moored down below the town itself due to the topography of the area.

There were several fishermen's homes here along with many wealthy ones owned by prosperous people. Greek was the major language spoken in the town. The population was mostly gentiles with a few Jews mixed in. A synagogue existed here amidst the rich homes and humble dwellings.

Tetrarch Phillip, another son of Herod the Great, ruled Gaulanitis as well as Trachonitis directly to the east. The Jordan River was the boundary between Galilee on the left side and Gaulanitis on the right. To the north lay the Roman province of Iturea.

John and his brother James along with Phillip were all from this place. They went ahead to prepare the way for the others. When these three disciples arrived at their hometown, they were met with excitement by many of the locals. They let everyone know that Jesus and his brother Judah would arrive shortly to provide healing, and then lecture to the masses. It was Jesus who was better known as the healer due to his growing reputation.

When the twins, along with the rest of the entourage, entered the outskirts of the small town, they set up their encampment in a secluded spot. Lush green grass was everywhere and looked like a green carpet spread across the land. It was an ideal location for them.

Once everything was in place, Jesus walked into the town and looked around. Immediately, he spotted an older blind man standing next to a light covered wall. A young man who looked like him was holding his arm in a supportive way. The Master Teacher went up to both of them. A linen cloth covered the blind man's eyes and was tied at the back of his bald head.

Hearing and sensing the presence of Jesus, the man begged and held his skinny arms out, "Jesus, please heal me."

Jesus stepped forward, grabbed the other arm and gave instructions, "Come with me outside the town where it is more private."

He, along with the young man, gently guided the old blind man out of town and under the trees in a private spot. The soft green grass could be felt beneath their sandals. The younger man, the son, let go of his father.

"Here. This spot will do." Jesus untied the cloth from around the man's head and then put spittle onto his fingertips. He put his fingers over the blind person's eyes and said, "Feel the healing. Know that your blindness is leaving. You will regain your sight."

The afflicted man yelled, "My eyes are burning. It hurts. I feel something going on inside both of my eyes."

"Open your eyes. What do you see?" asked Jesus.

"I can see blurry trees and some people but not clearly."

The healer put his fingertips onto the afflicted man's eyes again and then withdrew them. "Open your eyes again. Tell us what you see."

"I can see the trees clearly and several people standing nearby watching. The colours are beautiful. The sky is wonderful. I am cured. Bless you, Jesus."

"Go and do not tell anyone what has happened. Always be kind to others. Praise God in your heart."

"Thank you," mumbled the healed man. The son walked with him away from the town. A smile was on his youthful face. Of course, the healed man told everybody he met as soon as he could.

The Master Teacher joined the rest of his group and sat down on the soft grass beneath the shade of a large tree. Judah Thomas sat down beside him.

Matthew, the former tax collector and Judas Iscariot, their treasurer, glanced at each other, and then Matthew said, "Several people are waiting on the other side of the encampment. We will let them know that we are grateful for any donations as they come for healing treatments. We can let them think that Jesus is doing the healing on them. None of them have to know that both brothers will be doing the healing at the same time in different spots."

Judas Iscariot scratched his nose and mentioned, "These donations are needed to help support and feed us as we travel, and do our special work. If someone is too poor to pay, we will not turn them away. We provide charity and comfort to everyone who seeks our help."

"The money we receive from some of our female members covers most of our expenses, fortunately. Any donations we do receive will also help support our movement."

Both of them left the encampment, went around the trees and met the many people standing on the edge of town. Occasionally, the clinking of coins could be heard as a few of the potential patients paid a small donation and stepped forward.

Jesus and his brother began laying on of hands on many of the afflicted for several hours. Finally, by late afternoon, the crowds diminished and they took a well-deserved rest.

While Matthew and Judas the treasurer counted out the money between them, Judah Thomas talked to his twin, "I will go to the synagogue here and give a short sermon. The locals will not know that it is not you. I do not need to tell them. The message is important. I will come back after and then we can eat our supper by the campfires this evening."

He stood up, dusted off his cream colored robe, stomped the grass from his sandals and headed into the town to the local synagogue. Andrew, Simon, John, James and Phillip went with him for support.

As they stepped into the streets of the town, residents started to gather and follow them. When they reached the synagogue with its white columns and stone walls, a large group was standing about.

Judah Thomas smiled at them, walked through the doorway and into the synagogue. The interior of the structure became packed as the many people shuffled inside and found places to sit or stand. His brother Jesus was being asked to teach in synagogues throughout the region. It was the authority and power in his voice that drew the worshippers to him. Judah had the same power and loved to teach as well.

He stepped up to the altar, unrolled the scroll to the book of Isaiah and commenced reading, "The Spirit of the Lord is upon me, for he has anointed me to bring Good news to the poor. He has sent me to proclaim that captives will be released, that the blind will see, that the oppressed will be set free and that the time of the Lord's favor has come."

Then he sat down and said, "Today, this Scripture is fulfilled in your hearing."

The synagogue went quiet as the worshippers took in this audacious claim by Judah posing as Jesus. He had just proclaimed himself the Messiah or anointed one. People got angry and erupted. He and his disciples with him pushed past the listeners, and out the door onto the street. A mob started to form and pressed him towards a cliff nearby.

John, James, Andrew, Simon and Phillip forced back the incensed crowd, and tried to protect Judah Thomas. The mob could either stone him or throw him onto the stones below. Either way qualified as stoning in this land.

That is when Judah turned, glared at the angry crowd and yelled, "Get out of my way. Move now!" He pushed through them and kept walking. The five disciples joined him and formed a barrier around him to protect him. They made it through the streets to the outskirts of this small town and went to the numerous trees where their encampment was.

The mob held back and watched as the six men left the town. In twos and threes, they dispersed, and headed back into the streets and buildings of Bethsaida.

Jesus and the rest of the group observed the looks on the faces of Judah and the other five. It was obvious that something had gone awry. All the afflicted seeking healing had left and the members had the secluded place to themselves. Earlier, the twin brothers had performed healing on numerous individuals in separate locations near to each other. Again, most of the seekers had thought it was Jesus who performed the miraculous healings.

After Judah filled him in on the events at the synagogue, Jesus laughed, "Well, brother. It appears you have awakened and angered a sleeping dog. It now gnashes its teeth. I am glad you are making people think. You did what you were supposed to do."

Judah laughed too. He was almost thrown over a cliff to his death but he rose above it. The masses needed to know how important their work was.

Early that evening, they all went to a large open area covered with green grass. It overlooked the Sea of Galilee. There was lots of room here for the hundreds of followers that had come to hear Jesus give a sermon on the mount here. The sun would be up for a few hours yet.

Judah kept in the background out of the way and helped prepare some food for the masses. Bread and fish were the main staples provided for the gathering. Others, both male and female disciples, helped with the meal that would feed hundreds. Fish was cooked over fires and then sent out in baskets with bread.

From where they prepared the food, it looked like only a few loaves of bread and fish were there. Many of the followers kept seeing more and more bread, and fish being distributed out to the hungry people. Someone started a rumour that Jesus was feeding five hundred people with only five loaves of bread and five fish. This story made it through the crowd, and even filtered to the edges where some individuals stood listening and watching the sermon.

Joseph of Arimathea, a long-time member of the Great Sanhedrin council, as well as a faithful follower of Jesus and his brother, was amongst them. He became transfixed as the Master Teacher spoke his sermon with great power. A beautiful bluish white light completely covered Jesus and his light coloured robe as he talked.

The listeners were amazed by this light that surrounded him. They all gazed in awe and hung on his every word as he spoke, "Blessed are the poor in spirit, for theirs is the kingdom of heaven. Blessed are those who mourn, for they shall be comforted. Blessed are the meek, for they shall inherit the earth. Blessed are the merciful, for they shall receive mercy."

Jesus opened his arms, smiled out at everyone, and walked back and forth upon the mound. He continued, "You are the light of the world. Let your light shine before others, so that they may see your good works and give glory to your Father who is in heaven."

The Master Teacher kept talking, and covered subjects such as anger, lust, divorce, oaths, retaliation, love of your enemies and much more. Finally, he talked about what heaven above was like. He described beautiful gardens, flowers, angels and magnificent buildings. Some of these buildings were teaching and healing temples. He mentioned that the human soul of departed loved ones now existed in the heavenly realms above. He explained that it was a paradise waiting for everyone once they left the earthly realm. All were inspired and filled with happiness as he talked about heaven.

Finally, he stopped, looked at all about him and said, "Let us pray." He lowered his head, shut his eyes and pronounced the Lord's Prayer.

All the masses joined in this prayer. Love could be felt surging through the grass covered mound. For a moment, peace and love filled many hearts. There were a few lepers standing at the edge of the crowd who suddenly felt intense energy flowing through their afflicted bodies. In seconds, all of them were cured of their leprosy. Cries of joy rose from them as they touched their healed bodies, including their hands and faces. They all unwrapped the dirty linen cloths that covered their faces and gazed at each other in amazement.

Jesus also talked about the golden rule with great authority, "So, whatever you wish that others would do to you, do also to them, for this is the Law of the Prophets."

When Jesus finished his Sermon on the Mount, all were amazed. How could someone possess such power? The aura of light glowed around him. A beautiful smile graced his handsome face.

The fish and loaves continued to pour out to the listeners gathered here sitting on the grass or standing back under the shade of trees.

Once the sermon was done and the followers dispersed, Joseph of Arimathea went up the small mound to meet Jesus and Judah. For the last year or so, he had been to Nazareth and

Capernaum to learn from the brothers. He was an avid student of theirs.

Smiles and hugs were exchanged as they met again. The three of them sat down on the soft grass and started to talk.

"Your sermon was wonderful, Jesus." Joseph scratched his long nose and glanced at the Sea of Galilee in the near distance.

They were in an area close to both Capernaum and Bethsaida. It was serene and beautiful in this spot where they sat. The sun had already set and the stars twinkled in the night sky like a thousand small torch lights.

"Thank you, dear friend," answered Jesus. "I hope everyone got the message."

"Yes, I am sure they did. You must travel throughout the region and continue giving these inspiring sermons."

Joseph, an esteemed member of the Sanhedrin Council looked a bit nervous as if something was on his mind. "We need to talk about something important. I have to warn both of you."

Judah Thomas raised an eyebrow in concern. His brother had a frown on his bearded face.

Joseph waited a moment, gathered his thoughts, and spoke carefully and slowly, "Your reputations have grown tremendously. Even in Jerusalem you are both known for your healing gifts and speaking abilities. Especially you, Jesus. People know you are brothers but not twins. They would not know who was who if they were in your midst. All would believe it was Jesus they see."

"That does not seem to be anything to be concerned about. If I am speaking or doing the healing and the people think it is Jesus, so be it. I do not mind. Our work is what is truly important. We must touch the souls of others and heal the masses. We must open the hearts of many," proclaimed Judah as he met Joseph eye to eye.

The rich merchant from Jerusalem took in a deep breath, held it for a second, exhaled and said, "Joseph Caiaphas, the Chief High Priest, has heard about you two. He is a jealous, spiteful and dangerous man. He is very territorial, and considers Jerusalem and the surrounding area as part of his own spiritual authority. He would not take kindly to anyone intruding upon his territory. So, if you are both planning on visiting the city of

Jerusalem, be very careful where you tread and what you say. He has spies everywhere. Most importantly, he holds great power there and has the ear of Pontius Pilatus, the prefect of Judea."

"How would we be in danger if we only teach and heal while we are there?" asked Jesus who was a bit confused.

"Caiaphas does not believe you should be anywhere near Jerusalem. False Messiahs have come and gone, stirring up the masses. He likes to be in control with no problems. He worries about riots in the streets. If that were to happen, the Romans would come in, and end the riots with steel and blood in these very streets. When people worship at the temple and give money to the moneylenders there, he and his cronies make money. Also, they receive great donations from Jewish worshippers."

Joseph stopped for a moment to catch his breath. He then continued, "Caiaphas loves money and he loves his power. You two are a threat to that."

"Then, I guess, we will have to exercise great caution when we go to Jerusalem," announced Judah.

Joseph nodded his head in agreement. "The High Priest is old fashioned. He does not believe you have been sanctioned by God to do your work. In his opinion, you do not have the authority. So, it is very wise if you both tread lightly. Be careful. May you continue doing your spiritual work."

After that, the three of them along with the disciples ate a late supper and drank some red wine late into the night. Joseph after drinking a bit too much wine, laughed like a happy child, got up and headed back to Capernaum to stay in a room that he had rented earlier.

Jesus, Mary, Judah and all the group made up their beds under the stars, and were soon fast asleep. A soothing breeze blew through the trees. Everything was bathed in the glow of a half moon. It had been a wonderful day and their world was at peace for the moment.

Chapter Thirteen

John the Baptist had been imprisoned in a cell in Machaerus for almost two years. The time had gone by slowly for the prisoner. He wondered if Herod Antipas would ever release him.

Every day, the guards would bring John up out of his prison in the basement of a building in order to allow him to get some exercise. There was a water fountain in the lower city where he also bathed on a regular basis. The Baptist had finished a quick walk amongst the streets and started to wash himself off in the local fountain. The two guards watched his every move as he rinsed off his deeply muscled body.

Herod Antipas also known as Antipater came down from his palace accompanied by Jonathan, his captain of the guards and another guard. He spotted John leaning over the fountain splashing water over his bearded face. "Good morning, John. It is my birthday tomorrow. Good news. I have decided to release you as part of my birthday celebration. There will be dancing, drinking and feasting tomorrow evening."

John took a towel that was laying over the edge of the water fountain. He rubbed his body with the towel as he said, "Happy birthday, Herod. I am glad that you are finally releasing me. It is about time."

"I suppose it would be too much to ask you not to denounce my marriage anymore?"

"No. You would be wasting your time," replied John as he finished toweling off.

"Oh well," laughed Antipas. "I will announce your release during the celebration tomorrow night. May you go in peace, John."

"Peace be with you too, Herod." He watched as the Tetrarch turned and walked back up to his opulent palace. Jonathan and the other guard followed quietly behind their superior. John the Baptist was escorted back down into his dark and dirty cell again. He would believe he was finally free when Herod Antipas actually released him from this miserable place. Antipas had talked to him many times over the last year or so and listened to his teachings. He was intrigued by the Baptist but always held off releasing him. John knew that Herod Antipas held great ambitions. He wanted to be King of Judea like his father Herod the Great before him. John doubted that his jailer would ever be successful in the ambitious goal.

The next day, all of Herod Antipas's guests started to arrive for the birthday celebration. Rooms were given to each of the important guests. Dancers and musicians began setting up in the great dining room of the palace. Many of them practiced their songs and dance routines in the late afternoon.

Cooks and serving staff were very busy preparing all the food and wine for the many guests. Several rich merchants, upper level Roman administrators including Pontius Pilatus, the Prefect of Judea, had all arrived. Two Roman tribunes were included in the prominent guests.

Herodias, Antipater's wife, was excited that her daughter Salome would be doing a provocative dance tonight. Salome was a beautiful young woman with medium dark skin, lovely eyes and a voluptuous body. Her performance would be the highlight of the evening's entertainment. Herodias knew Herod would be thrilled by Salome's dance tonight. That would be when she would lay her trap on her unsuspecting husband. An evil smile graced the beautiful face of Herodias as she thought about this.

Herod Antipas was in for a major surprise. What a birthday present for him. He had told her of his plan to release John the Baptist tonight. The only release Herodias wanted for John was his release from his worthless life. Yes, it would be an amazing evening.

The numerous servants lit all the oil lamps as the evening descended upon the palace. Some musicians started playing at the far end of the triclinium or dining room. The honoured guests were seated on dining couches with wine on tables in front of them. The serving staff began to bring in delicious foods on silver plates. Chicken, fish and other delicacies were on the plates. The smell of various dishes filled the large dining room.

As the gathering laughed, drank, and ate, numerous half-naked dancers, male and female, appeared on the marble floor directly in front of the celebrants. Dark skinned and muscular men danced, and gyrated dressed only in loin clothes. The females, light and dark skinned, and bare breasted, joined in the dance. All of the dancers swayed back and forth to the drums and pipes. Torch lights from sconces on the stone walls reflected off the glistening skin of the dancers.

The crowd grew louder as the red and white wine flowed. Laughter filled the huge room. The food was delicious with all the herbs used in the preparations.

As the evening progressed, more food and wine was consumed by all. The musicians kept playing and then one by one, the dancers left the marble floor that was used as a stage. All of them disappeared behind stately columns and palace walls. The celebrants noticed the shift and gazed out at the floor before them. The musicians were still in the distance against an inner palace wall.

Suddenly, Herodias, slightly intoxicated, wandered over to the musicians and in a husky voice gave instructions, "Stop playing now. When my daughter Salome walks through those two pillars, begin playing the music for the dance of the seven veils. Start off slowly, and then speed up until my daughter dances and gyrates quickly. Then, when she is finished, stop the music abruptly." She quickly pointed at the columns nearby.

A tall, slender grey haired man who was in charge of the musicians nodded his head in understanding. "Of course, we will do a great job for Salome."

Herod Antipas and all the half-drunken guests looked at the musicians and Herodias. There was a sense of anticipation in the great dining chamber now.

Herodias walked slowly and provocatively towards her husband who was sprawled out on a dining couch. "Herod, my husband. As promised, my daughter Salome will dance the dance of the seven veils for you and all of your guests as a birthday gift. She will do the full and complete dance for your pleasure, husband."

Upon hearing this, Pontius Pilatus, the Tribune Publius and all the others clapped, and cheered loudly. Smiles were on everyone's faces. This dance was very sensual and erotic. Some of the oil lamps were extinguished by servants as per earlier instructions setting the scene upon the large floor. The crowd went quiet.

Suddenly, a beautiful raven haired woman walked seductively between two white columns. She wore several pieces of cloth over her lovely body. They were extensive veils of various colours that covered most of her exquisite form. Even with the cloth over top, her body could be made out beneath.

The musicians started playing flutes gently, and a drummer drummed slowly and rhythmically. Salome began her dance. She twirled once letting her long dark hair flow out. The light of the lamps and torches reflected off her beautiful hair. Her well-developed body swayed slowly back and forth. She smiled seductively at her stepfather. Salome was becoming his seductress, promising a night of pure ecstasy for him. Antipas, who had lusted after her lovely mother, now lusted after the daughter. Passion and desire filled his hungry eyes.

She lifted a light green veil and held it just below her exotic eyes. Then, in a practiced move, she threw it out toward the Tribune Publius. He grabbed it greedily and laughed with delight. This beautiful creature played to the audience. She entertained each and every one of them. Every time she lifted her arms or moved a shapely leg, her stomach and legs would be revealed beneath the material. Salome had everyone's undivided attention.

She twirled, and swayed again and again. The spectators were awestruck. She threw off another veil that landed just below the dining couches. Her bare feet moved across the stone floor with skill. Salome's supple right breast was fully exposed. She smiled knowing this and continued her erotic dance. All the men stared at her with lust in their eyes; especially her step-father, Antipas. He licked his lips with delight. She worked provocatively across the floor removing veil after veil. One of her last remaining veils was thrown at Pontius Pilatus who reached for it with great anticipation. His wife, Claudia sat beside him with her fists clenched tight. She was one of the few who did not enjoy the dancing beauty before them. Finally, Salome moved towards Herod Antipas, and threw off the seventh and last veil exposing the other breast. The lower part of her body was barely covered. Sweat glistened on her. Her chest heaved up and down from the exertion. Antipas grabbed the purple veil and clutched it to him. This dance was a wonderful gift to him for his birthday. He anticipated even more joy later from Salome. Her eyes said it all as she looked at him.

Most of the food had been consumed but the wine still flowed freely. All the celebrants were in various states of drunkenness.

"Salome," proclaimed Herod. "I will give you anything you want, up to half my kingdom. What do you want, dear child?"

Salome was not sure what to say even though her mother had talked to her earlier. She glanced over at her mother, Herodias who stepped off the dining couch. She walked toward her nearly naked daughter. Soon, the two of them were in deep conversation. A smile covered both their faces as they came to a mutual agreement. Herodias went back up to the couch and sat down beside her drunken husband.

The daughter of Herodias took in a deep breath and relaxed. She had recovered from the exotic dance. "I want the head of John the Baptist on a silver platter," she announced and threw back her radiant black hair.

The room went dead quiet as everyone absorbed the unusual request.

"Wha…" exclaimed Antipas. He scratched his head and looked at her in disbelief. "No, that I cannot do."

"But you promised. You said I could have half of your kingdom. That is my wish. That is all I want. Give me the head of John the Baptist on a silver platter. Now!"

Herod Antipas mumbled and shook his head. He was torn. He did not want to kill John the Baptist but he would lose face in front of his important guests if he did not honour her request.

Finally, Antipas or Antipater relinquished. He yelled, "Jonathan, come here. Bring the executioner with you." In a matter of moments, the captain of the guard stepped into the dining room. Beside him stood a giant of a man holding a large sword in his black hands. The muscles rippled under his white tunic.

"Jonathan, go to the cell of John the Baptist and have your executioner behead him. Then, bring his severed head on a silver platter to this dining room. Do it now as quickly as possible. Go!" The captain of the guard nodded his head in assent and then turned. He and Ahab, the executioner, left the room, and proceeded down to the lower city where the Baptist was imprisoned.

Jonathan with the executioner and two guards behind him walked down the stairs that led to the Baptist's cell. At the bottom, they could see the powerful John holding onto the bars of the cell with his hands. He glared at all of them. Disgust was in his eyes. "John, we have come for you," said Jonathan as he reached for his sword. He used the other hand to gather a set of iron keys. Nervously, he put the proper key into the keyhole and turned it. The cell door creaked and then opened. He may not of liked the Baptist but he did not relish would he had to do.

"Have you come to release me? Did Herod agree to free me as he promised on his birthday?"

"No. We have come to release you from your pitiful life." He nodded over at Ahab to proceed. The huge black man stepped into the cell and reached for John the Baptist. The other two guards assisted by grabbing John's arms. John struggled against the giant bear of a man but to no avail. The Baptist may have been a strong, powerful man but he was no match for Ahab. The other guards made his struggle even more futile. In seconds, Ahab and the guards dragged John out of the cell into the open area. As the captain of the guard sat on the Baptist, the executioner lifted his menacing sword. In one smooth motion, the blade sliced through the neck of John like a hot knife through liquid. The severed head of John rolled across the dirty room, bounced against a wall and then stared back at Jonathan. The eyes and mouth still moved back and forth silently in the severed head. Then the movement stopped. Blood was splayed all over the floor and wall of the area.

Jonathan carried the severed head of the Baptist into the dining room on a silver platter. All eyes were on the horrid sight. The unseeing eyes of John stared out at nothing. Herod felt sick to his stomach. His deceitful wife, Herodias beamed with pure joy. Blood lust filled her whole being. Her devious plan had worked. That disgusting man was now dead. John would never badmouth her again. Jonathan stepped around the table, and laid the silver platter at the feet of the Tetrarch Antipas and stepped back. He quickly left the huge room.

"Servants. Servants. Remove the head of John the Baptist from my sight. Throw his head onto the dung heap outside," screeched Herod. Two male servants came forward and one bent down to pick up the unwelcome silver platter. They soon left with the head as per Herod's order. The celebrants forgot about the incident and went back to drinking more wine.

Herod let the red wine dull his senses. He focused on Salome and the possibility of a night of passion with her. The birthday party continued into the evening. Eventually, all the guests retired to luxurious quarters for the night.

* * *

Jesus, Mary Magdalene and Judah were on the road walking back to their former home in Nazareth. They wanted to spend some relaxing time with their family. The twins had not seen their mother in several weeks now. It was time for a break from teaching and healing.

The disciple Andrew spotted them on the road ahead. He had just returned from the palace of Machaerus in the south. He needed to share some important news with the brothers. He waved at all of them and called out, "Jesus, Mary and Judah. Wait up. I need to talk to you."

He ran several steps and then stopped in front of all three of them. He caught his breath and then announced, "John the Baptist is dead. Herod Antipas had him beheaded like a rabbit. His body is still in Machaerus minus his head. I think the head is in a dung heap. I am saddened and very angry at the same time."

The three listeners were stunned by the awful news. No one spoke for a moment as they all digested this information.

Jesus spoke up first, "What? Is this a joke? John has been executed?"

"Yes. An executioner lopped off his head like a rabbit as I said. Someone needs to claim the remains and make sure that

John has a proper burial. Herod is a disgusting pig!" Andrew spit the words out. Spittle hung from his lips.

Jesus, Mary and Judah all started to cry as the news was fully absorbed by them. Emotional pain wracked their bodies. Eventually, the tears subsided.

Judah, after regaining his composure, said, "Andrew, make arrangements for some of you to go to Machaerus and retrieve John's remains. Find a cart and a donkey to transport his body back to where he baptized the many. This is where it should be buried with respect."

Mary Magdalene wiped the tears from her eyes, nodded in agreement and caught the gaze of her husband. She could feel the sadness within Jesus too.

Jesus also wiped his tears off, with a hand, used a sleeve of a tunic to dry his face and then repeated the instructions of his brother, "Yes. Find a few disciples and bring his body back to where he baptized followers by the Jordan River."

Jesus gave a few silver coins to Andrew for necessary expenses. They then all hugged a sad goodbye. The first disciple of the twin's went on to Capernaum to find help with his sorrowful task.

The brothers and Mary kept on the road, and headed back to Nazareth to be with their family. This would be the ideal place for all of them to grieve the loss of John the Baptist. Above on a branch of a huge tree, a black bird sat staring at them. It was a belief that the sighting of a black bird was an omen for telling of death. The sign or omen sat on the branch and kept staring at them.

Chapter Fourteen

They spent almost two weeks with the family in Nazareth. It was wonderful. The meals, the laughter and the sharing recharged their souls.

Mother Mary loved having the three of them there. She enjoyed walking about the area with Jesus and Judah. Her walks with Mary, the wife of Jesus, were especially pleasing for her. They would talk about herbs and family.

On the thirteenth day, they were ready to leave their former home and continue with their ministry. The twins were both anxious about travelling to Bethany near Jerusalem. Their dear friend Lazarus lived in this very small village with his two younger sisters, Maria and Rebecca. For some unexplained reason, they needed to visit him as soon as possible. Intuitive feelings kept tugging at both of them.

Just before they left for Bethany, Andrew the disciple showed up in Nazareth. Immediately, he told them about retrieving the body of John the Baptist.

"Did you have any problems, Andrew?" asked Judah as he loaded a donkey up with a few supplies. He adjusted a leather cinch and looked directly at the disciple.

"No. The guards at Machaerus turned over John's remains. Someone even found the severed head in a dung heap and brought it to us."

"As you are aware, Andrew, my brother and I tried to visit our cousin John while he was imprisoned at Machaerus. Unfortunately, Antipas gave orders that we were not allowed to visit. We were turned back. It is sad that we could not see John the Baptist before he was murdered," Jesus explained with intense sadness in his voice. He felt a total loss.

"Yes. At least, you and Judah tried to visit him. Antipas can be a real bastard." Andrew was sympathetic. "We buried John in a secret place near to where he baptized hundreds of followers. We thought this was best so that no one would disturb his remains," Andrew kept talking to all of them.

Jesus, Mary and Judah nodded their heads in complete agreement. They all hoped that John the Baptist would now be at peace in heaven.

Mary walked up to the disciple and asked, "What are you going to do now? Are you heading back to Capernaum?"

"Yes. I need to gather our group and join you again on your journey."

"Great. We will wait for all of you near here on the road that leads to Jerusalem," announced Mary. "Then we can all go together to Bethany. My mother in law, Mary will be joining us too."

Chapter Fifteen

"Lazarus is dead," cried Maria as she met them all near the edge of Bethany. "He died nearly three days ago." Tears ran down her cheeks. Her hair was a mess. Her sister Rebecca was beside her and could barely speak. Both were grieving for their beloved brother.

"What happened?" both Jesus and Judah asked in unison. They were confused by the reception from Maria and Rebecca along with all the people gathered here.

Maria, the eldest sister, collected her breath and then explained, "Lazarus was not feeling well. So, he lay down outside by the front of our home under a shade tree for a rest. He was there for several hours and did not wake up. Both Rebecca and I tried to rouse him but he did not open his eyes or respond."

She started sobbing. Mary Magdalene put her arms around her to comfort her. She cried a bit longer and then stopped abruptly. "We checked for life signs but could find no pulse nor could we hear his heartbeat. His breathing had ceased. We knew that our beloved brother was dead."

Rebecca, nearby, could be heard crying quietly. Her thin shoulders shook.

"Where is the body of Lazarus?" queried Jesus. "We need to go there now."

Judah had seen that look on his brother's face before. He knew it was imperative to listen to Jesus.

Rebecca stopped crying and with red eyes, pointed towards a small hill to the right. Some trees blocked the view. "Lazarus is buried in a rock tomb there."

Everyone went to the tomb area. Jesus commanded, "Remove the rock. Roll it back!"

Three younger men stepped forward and slowly rolled the round rock back exposing the entrance to the tomb of Lazarus. The effort caused them to perspire.

Jesus looked at his brother standing beside him and said, "Judah, you stay out here and send energy to the situation within the tomb. Use the techniques we were taught in Egypt. I will enter the tomb and do what I must. Angels will help us as we focus."

The Master Teacher quickly entered the entrance to the dark tomb. He let his eyes adjust to the dimness. Against the far wall lay the body of Lazarus wrapped in linen on a shelf. Jesus could swear the body of his friend breathed for a split second. Above the body, the soul of Lazarus floated in a bluish white light. The soul was in the form of Lazarus and had an ethereal essence to it. The Egyptians had taught him and his brother about the human soul, and how a silver cord of energy kept it attached to the physical body for several days prior to final death.

Jesus walked closer and commanded the soul of Lazarus to return into the body. "Lazarus, my friend, hear my voice. Come back into your body now."

He raised both arms and touched the soul of his friend. Slowly, the ethereal mist started to lower. A bright white light formed beside Jesus. This was an angel come to assist. Between the light from the helping angel and the hands of the Master Teacher, Lazarus's soul settled evenly and easily into the linen covered body.

Jesus heard a gasp and then his friend started to breathe slowly. The cloth covered chest of Lazarus rose and fell. His body moved slightly.

Moments later, Jesus and Lazarus who was partially unwrapped from his linens, stepped out of the rock tomb and into the light of day.

Judah smiled as he knew what had transpired. He had focused, and sent energy to his brother and Lazarus as instructed. Many of the people gathered gasped and put their hands over their open mouths. The sight was unbelievable to many. A miracle had happened. Lazarus had been raised from the dead.

Soon, a few men started shouting, "Lazarus has been raised from the dead." These men overwhelmed with emotion and joy started running down a path towards Jerusalem on the other side of the Kidron Valley. The twin of Jesus could hear their shouts of joy fading as they ran to the ancient city. Jesus helped Lazarus to walk forward. Maria and Rebecca rushed to hug their brother.

Joseph Caiaphas, the high priest was sitting on a balcony of his opulent home reading a scroll. He looked up as he heard the excited voices of some men shouting, "Lazarus has been raised from the dead by Jesus. He performed a miracle. Lazarus is alive."

Caiaphas went to the edge of the balcony and leaned against a supporting wall. He gazed down into the street below. About four or five men were running down the street still shouting about Lazarus being raised from the dead. The high priest was not happy to hear this announcement. He walked back to the open doorway and found a temple guard standing nearby. "You. I want you to find Simon my chief spy and bring him to me as soon as possible. Now, go and find him."

The high priest went back to the edge of the balcony and looked out over this part of Jerusalem. He considered it his domain. He had become very rich in this prominent position. He ran his hand through his thick salt and pepper hair, and glanced down at his expensive robe. Gold thread shimmered in the fabric. Caiaphas was in great shape for man of middle years and took great pride in his physique. He was above average in height but seemed taller when he commanded a room with his powerful voice.

He heard footsteps coming down the hallway and turned as Simon, his chief spy strode out on to the spacious balcony. "Ah Simon, I need you to keep an eye on someone for me. The man is a potential trouble maker and I need him watched discreetly. I know you can do this," he fingered his neatly trimmed beard as he spoke.

Simon was a tall man with massive shoulders. He had been a soldier in the past and still carried a military gait when he walked. A scar ran down the right side of his still handsome face. He had intelligent brown eyes and focused them on his employer. "Yes, I can do that for you. I have a few assistants to help with the detail."

"Good. I need you to keep a watchful eye on a man called Jesus. He is a teacher and rabbi from the Galilee region. He has quite a following there and it seems to be spreading here into Jerusalem. He draws great crowds wherever he goes. His influence over the people gives me concern."

"Fear not, sir. We will keep an eye on him for the next week or so. I will have my men take turns observing this Jesus and his movements. Where is he now?"

"I believe he is over the other side of the Kidron Valley on the Mount of Olives. There is a man named Lazarus that lives there with his sisters in the village of Bethany. I have seen this man at the temple a few times over the years. I even heard him speak about Jesus to a few people in the great court a few times. He claims to be a friend of this rabbi or teacher."

"Simon," added Caiaphas. "Jesus is reported to have performed miracles in Galilee. Healing lepers and the blind are some of the reports I have received back from other sources. Apparently, he has just raised his friend Lazarus from the dead. Or at least that is what a few men just shouted as they ran through the streets of the city. Let me know if he performs any more miracles. I need to know. Now go and get back to me every few days with some information."

Simon bent his large head and nodded at the high priest. The chief spy possessed a shaggy head of flaming red hair. He would stand out in any crowd. It was good thing that his men were doing the spying and not him. "As you wish, priest Caiaphas. I will see you in two days with information about this man."

He turned, walked through the open portal and proceeded down the hall of Caiaphas's stately home.

The high priest sat down on a cushion covered sofa and pondered the situation. What would he do with Jesus? How could he eliminate this man if needed? He looked down at his perfectly trimmed fingernails and the expensive rings that adorned the fingers. He was meticulous about his appearance. His personal barber had just trimmed his hair and beard the other day.

Chapter Sixteen

Lazarus sat on a wooden bench in front of a large table. He was enjoying the shade of the oak tree above. Occasionally, a gentle breeze blew across his face. It felt great to be alive. He noticed his two sisters serving food, and some drinks to the disciples of Jesus and Judah. The smell of freshly baked bread wafted towards him. Lazarus was actually getting hungry. He waved at Maria and yelled, "Bring me some food and drink, sister, please."

Maria waved back, and headed over to where he was with a plate of food in one hand and a glass of wine in the other. She set it down on the table and smiled at him, "I am glad you have your appetite back, Lazarus."

"Yes. It feels wonderful to be hungry and experience the wonders of life again. I feel truly blessed." He raised his arms above his head and yawned.

"I must head back and help Rebecca with all our new friends. Oh, I see Jesus and Judah returning from their walk. They both must be famished." She walked briskly back to the other tables and chairs where everyone was seated feasting. It was only a dozen steps from where Lazarus sat enjoying his meal.

The twin brothers, who were both called rabbis due to their teaching abilities, squeezed in among their happy disciples. Rebecca brought them both a plate full of delicious food along with a glass of red wine. They were soon busy devouring the meals that were before them.

Lazarus wolfed down his grilled chicken, cooked onions, olives, bread and honeyed cakes. He rose slowly and headed over to join the rest of them. He had to sit at the end of the long table with an empty glass in his hands. He surveyed the group before him. Along with the inner circle of twelve and the wife of Jesus, a few other men and women were there.

The sun's rays were starting to cast a golden aura upon the land. Lazarus could almost imagine himself plucking gold off the leaves of the trees and grass. The evening was becoming magical. Since he was still weak, he asked, "I have a favour to ask. Would someone here start a fire for us in the fire pit over there?" He raised his thin arm and pointed to the darkened spot that was close to two ancient olive trees.

"Sure. No problem," volunteered Matthew. He glanced at Andrew who was beside him. Andrew was wiping off his meal with the sleeve of his old robe. The robe had seen better days.

Both of the men got up from the crowded table and started foraging for firewood nearby. There was lots of dry wood pieces on the Mount of Olives. In no time at all, they gathered enough firewood and set it down beside the fire pit. Judah picked up a torch that had just been lit by one of the sisters of Lazarus and went over to help. Soon, a large campfire started to crackle as the dry wood was tossed into it.

One by one, the group left the dining table area and sauntered over to the roaring fire. Everyone found seats on either the grass or chairs that were brought over. As they all made themselves comfortable, Maria and Rebecca brought over more wine. The laughter that began during the feast was contagious and continued here.

The sun dipped below the horizon and soon stars appeared in the sky. It was like an invisible hand had lit tiny lamps in the darkening sky. The fire blazed in the fire pit as everyone continued to drink wine.

It was during these times that Jesus loved to teach, and answer questions from his disciples and followers as they all gathered about the fire.

Jesus and his twelve closest disciples, and Lazarus and his sisters, sat about the roaring campfire along with several other followers, both male and female. Mary Magdalene, his beautiful wife and constant companion sat beside him.

The flow of the fire glistened off her long dark hair. The light reflected in her eyes as she gazed into the flames.

Jesus gave her a gentle kiss on the lips, and turned and looked about the fire at everyone. He smiled and said, "I want to talk to all of you about two things this evening. I want to explain what happened to Lazarus and then talk about reincarnation."

All eyes were now upon his handsome face. "The human soul is eternal and is attached to the heavenly fields above. Our bodies are houses or temples that our souls inhabit during our lives. At the time of death, our souls, our true selves will leave the physical body, float above it and then ascend to the heavenly fields above. In essence, we vibrate to a higher level."

The fire crackled and the flames rose slightly. The light was reflected on all faces.

"What are the heavenly fields like?" asked Matthew as he leaned forward a bit.

"Ah. The heavenly fields above are very beautiful and peaceful. Words cannot describe the beauty that abounds there. When our human souls leave this earth, we return home to heaven or the heavenly fields. This happens just shortly after the physical death of the body."

The Master Teacher took a moment to collect this thoughts. He smiled and continued, "My friend Lazarus was not dead yet. His body was in what is called a coma. The Egyptians taught Judah and me about this in the school at Heliopolis. Basically, the human body is near death in a very deep state of sleep or unconsciousness. It appears that the body is dead to many people that observe it."

"In reality, the human soul is floating in and out of the human form. The soul has not yet returned to heaven. Lazarus was in this state. With the help of an angel, we were able to bring his soul back into his body. To many of you, it would seem that he rose from the dead. In reality, his eternal soul went back into the physical body. He regained consciousness and is now among us." Everyone murmured in agreement as Jesus stopped talking for a brief moment.

"Let us return to the subject of reincarnation. When the human soul returns to the heavenly fields after the physical body has died, the soul will remain here for some time. This soul will meet loved ones that have passed over before and reflect upon the life that has just ended. Angels and special spirit guides or teachers will counsel the soul here. The human soul will rest and enjoy the time here in heaven."

Jesus looked up at the many stars in the evening sky and then continued, "When the soul is ready, it will go before a special council of elders called the Elohim. On this great council in heaven, sits many wise beings of light. They will discuss many options with this soul. A plan will be arranged for the soul to return to earth for another lifetime. This plan is for the greatest spiritual growth of that particular soul. This soul along with the advice of the elders will decide what country to be born in, what parents to choose and even what sex to be in the upcoming lifetime. Once this plan or soul contract is made, the human soul will vibrate down to heaven, and hover in and out of a pregnant mother. Finally, at the time of birth, the soul will enter into the new born and become one."

All eyes were upon Jesus and he kept speaking, "Thus, another lifetime on earth has begun for the human soul. This cycle of life, death and rebirth will continue until that soul has become truly enlightened."

Matthew cleared his throat and asked, "What happens when the soul becomes enlightened?"

"Very good question, Matthew. Once the soul is enlightened, the cycle of reincarnation ends. The human soul has learnt its lessons and can now remain in heaven forever."

Everybody was quiet as they digested this amazing information.

That night after the fire had died down, all the people gathered here outside the home of Lazarus, and his sisters, Maria and Rebecca found places to sleep. Jesus and Mary were given a private area inside the home. The night grew later and all found sleep easily. The copious amounts of wine had helped. The stars shone and the moon glowed above the Mount of Olives. A magical day had come to an end.

Chapter Seventeen

"Riding into Jerusalem on a borrowed donkey may be very dangerous," warned Judas Iscariot, as he looked around at everyone gathered in the garden near Bethany. "But it will be the fulfilment of the prophecy found in the book of Zechariah."

"Yes, I believe this is part of my destiny," stated Jesus confidently, as his eyes pierced deep inside the souls of each of the disciples, one by one.

Matthew, the former tax collector, spoke up quickly before anyone else, "Master, you are giving the message that you are the Messiah and King of Israel!"

Voices erupted in argument. Even, Judah Thomas, his twin brother was uncomfortable with this audacious plan. He stood up and waved the group to silence with his hands, and yelled, "Be quiet. Let me speak. I may not agree with my brother but the plan does have some merit. It allows us to reach the hearts and souls of many more people."

"But the masses are only looking for a messianic figure who will deliver us from our Roman oppressors: not a spiritual teacher and healer," bellowed Simon, the former fisherman.

The lively discussion fired up again. Fists were shaking, fingers pointing, and arms were waving up and down. Shouts of, "This is madness!" on one side, to "This is brilliant!" and many opinions in between were expressed.

Andrew, the first disciple, stepped back from the melee, waved his arms frantically. He looked like a tall, agitated skinny bird. "Be quiet! Silence now. Listen to me. Listen."

The voices settled down as all eyes turned to him. A hush fell upon the gathering. "This is an amazing opportunity for us. The timing is perfect. As long as we are careful and give hope to the masses, we will be safe; we will be protected. We promote spirituality and not a religion…"

Simon interrupted, shook his hairy head slightly and played with his beard. He mumbled, "I do not know if this plan will work over time. But, if you feel that strongly about it, I will not stand in anyone's way."

"I still think this plan is fool hardy. What if you fail in your attempt?" He glanced at Jesus out of the corner of his eye. "Should we 'turn the other cheek' as you always say?" He started to laugh from deep down inside. Slowly, everyone else did too.

The phrase 'turn the other cheek' was considered a great insult. If a man used his clean hand to strike the person in front of him then the intended victim would, simply, turn the other cheek towards his assailant, thereby forcing the man to use his dirty hand; the one that he wiped his behind with.

Everyone roared for a few moments. This broke the tension.

Joseph of Arimathea, a long-time supporter and secret disciple of the Master Jesus, put in another visit that evening. He approached the group gathered amidst the trees near the home of Lazarus. Judah Thomas greeted the rich merchant with a warm smile as the member of the Great Sanhedrin threw off his mantle onto the ground.

A mantle was an outer cloak worn over other clothing. While it was used mainly as a means to keep warm, it also served another purpose. For some people, it represented a symbol of authority.

Everyone stepped back in a respectful manner and let Joseph walk through their midst towards the area where Jesus waited quietly.

"Your eyes show fear and worry," said Jesus peering at his mentor and secret follower. A solitary torch light flickering nearby reflected the scene dimly. "I know why you have come."

"Master Jesus, are you mad? Have you lost your mind?" The wealthy merchant twisted his long hair in a nervous manner. He bit his lip and continued, "I have just come from an emergency meeting of the council ordered by Caiaphas, the High Priest. He is very close to having you arrested. The only reason he has not done so is because of your large following and fame. He does not want to cause a riot. You must be careful that you do not provoke him in any way."

Jesus smiled at his long-time supporter. Joseph had contributed funds to the movement over the last few years. The Master Teacher took a deep breath, sighed and proceeded to tell the rich merchant of his plan for the next morning. When he finished, he looked straight into the eyes of Joseph.

The rich merchant and member of the Great Sanhedrin had his mouth open in amazement. It seemed an eternity before he finally spoke, "Now I know you have lost your sanity. Your plan is tantamount to proclaiming yourself King of the Jews. This action would open you up to a possible arrest by Caiaphas, or at least, a watchful eye by the Roman authorities."

Joseph shook his head in disbelief as he continued, "I cannot protect you from the powers that be. If you follow through with your madness to ride into Jerusalem on a donkey, then this action will be reported back to Caiaphas, the High Priest. He has spies that work for him. I think one of them is watching you and waiting for the right moment to pass on information to his employer. You may be signing your own death warrant."

Jesus was very passionate as he replied, "I know that, my friend. But it is my destiny. I will follow through with my plan. That is why I am here on the earth now. I must allow my destiny to unfold."

He opened his palms up and gazed towards the heavens above. "God speaks to me through his angels. This is what I must do. Nothing will stop me."

Joseph gazed up at the night sky too and then down at his sandaled feet. "It is obvious that you have made up your mind. Oh well, let us leave it in the Creator's hands. There is something else I need to discuss with you, if I may, Master Jesus?"

"Yes. What is it, Joseph?" asked Jesus as he stared off into the distance.

The rich merchant cleared his throat and said, "I have heard you say it is easier for a rope to go through the eye of a needle than it is for a rich man to go to heaven. If that is true, will I never see heaven?"

103

The Master Teacher laughed breaking the tension. He explained patiently, "For many years, I have observed fishermen in Capernaum mending their nets. They would take a small piece of rope, and carefully thread it through a large needle and then tie it off. From there, a hole in the net could be repaired as the fisherman used the needle and rope to sew. It may have been a challenge to repair a net in this manner but not impossible."

"A rich man that has a good heart and a kind soul will get to heaven. You are a very kind and loving man, Joseph. Fear not. You will see heaven after you depart this earth." He smiled fondly at the rich man who stood before him in this private area.

"Thank you. I feel much better." A few tears glistened in the eyes of Joseph. "I must leave you now and return home. Remember, Caiaphas has spies everywhere and he may very well be watching me too."

Both student and teacher warmly embraced. The member of the Great Sanhedrin put on his cloak, walked past all the disciples and headed down an old pathway into the Kidron Valley which was just below the city of Jerusalem.

The torches flickered a bit as a slight wind picked up. Jesus used his arms to rub his arms in order to rub off the slight chill that he felt. He wondered, was it a chill caused by the weather or by how he felt inside?

That night, a half moon shone down on the Mount of Olives as Jesus and his disciples slept.

Chapter Eighteen

"Hosanah! Hosanah!" shouted the crowd of followers as Jesus rode on the back of a borrowed donkey into Jerusalem. His brother and a few disciples walked alongside the Master Teacher while the rest followed just behind. The rumours had spread that Jesus would enter the city triumphantly as per the prophecy. Thus, a large gathering cheered him on and lay palm fronds in front of the borrowed beast. It was a lovely day and the sun shone down upon the eventful scene. Many people reached out to him to touch his robe in hopes of being healed or at least blessed by this amazing man.

His twin brother, Matthew and Judas Iscariot tried to keep the excited mob away by gently pushing them back. It was almost an overwhelming task as they walked on both sides of the donkey. Hands were reaching and begging to be touched by Jesus.

Andrew and his fiery tempered brother Simon had thrown two cloaks over the back of the borrowed donkey so Jesus would have a semblance of comfort as he sat on its back.

Along with palms, some of the multitude had also thrown cloaks in front of the donkey and the procession. Some yelled "Messiah" and "Jesus is the Messiah" as Jesus and the disciples headed into the ancient city. There were even a few "King of the Jews" comments shouted out.

The crowd was ecstatic and joyous as the group entered. It was apparent that the great teacher and healer was adored by them.

Simon, the spy for the High Priest Caiaphas, leaned against a straggly palm tree and watched the scene. A slight smile graced his face as he thought about reporting this to his superior. He knew a generous reward would be given for this valuable information. After all, the High Priest was a very wealthy man and had no problem being generous when it suited his needs.

Jesus sitting on the borrowed donkey rode into the ancient city with a smile on his face. He waved at the adoring multitude. He was very pleased with the great turnout.

They carried on through the crowded streets and made their way to the Holy Temple. King Herod's temple was an architectural marvel, spacious with many numerous stone columns forming a great colonnade on all sides. It surrounded the large open courtyard and area within. The colonnaded areas offered some shade from the warmth of the sun. Several people were scattered throughout this area taking advantage of the shade there.

Jesus had left the borrowed donkey along with the cloaks just outside on a street below. They had to walk up steps to enter the massive complex. He, Andrew, Simon and the rest of the group including his twin brother, walked between two stone columns, and stopped there. There were few people here so Jesus decided to give his sermon here in the relative shade and protection of this colonnaded spot.

He and his disciples looked out onto the huge courtyard called the Court of the Gentiles. There were Jew and non-Jew, dark skinned men from Africanus, medium skinned Greeks, and lighter skinned people with blonde hair and blue eyes. Jerusalem was a metropolitan city with the Holy Temple, circus and Roman baths within its boundaries.

Mary Magdalene, his wife, stood beside him holding his hand. She was his constant companion and confidante. He felt very blessed.

Jesus released her hand and stepped forward. Many of his followers had found shade in the portico under the stone columns. Some sat on the floor, some leaned against available columns and a few stood nearby. There were even a few people standing in the sun.

"Friends, brothers and sisters, I bring you a great message. Heaven above is beautiful. If you can think of a glorious garden or park on earth, then you can imagine what heaven really looks like. It is even more wonderful and beautiful." The Master Teacher took a deep breath, looked up at the huge crowd that had now gathered around him and continued, "Once

106

your immortal soul leaves this earth, you will experience wonders."

Jesus was now repeating the sermon that he had given in Galilee near the Sea of Galilee. Many people referred to it as the Sermon on the Mount.

The listeners were fascinated by the sermon Jesus gave. His vivid description of heaven filled them with hope and happiness. The crowd grew even larger just before he finished.

After delivering this amazing sermon, he and his twin brother did healing on several people that were there. There was no charge for this but donations were gratefully accepted. These donations along with the funds that Mary Magdalene and Sarah, another female disciple provided, helped the movement immensely.

Once the crowd thinned out and all the healing sessions were completed, Jesus decided to visit the Siloam Pool nearby. The ancient pool was located outside the city walls on the Southeast part of the city.

"Heal me. Heal me, Jesus!" beseeched the elderly blind man standing in the Siloam Pool. He had been blind since birth. The man had his arms out in a pleading manner. The Master Teacher removed his sandals and stepped into the lukewarm water. He scooped up water into his hands and poured it over the top of the blind man's head. He spat into his fingers, rubbed them together and then put his fingertips of both hands onto the man's closed eyelids. "My eyes hurt. They are burning," cried the blind man.

A bluish white light now glowed from the fingertips of Jesus. The light also shone on the blind man's face. A few moments later, the mysterious light vanished.

Jesus removed his fingers and stepped back. "Open your eyes. Then go bathe in the pool again."

The elderly man blinked, looked around and exclaimed, "I can see colours and shapes moving in front of my eyes." He followed Jesus's command and bathed in the Pool of Siloam. Everyone including the disciples watched him. "I can see even better now."

The Pool of Siloam was the only permanent water source for the city of Jerusalem. It was fed by the waters of the Gihon

Spring diverted through Hezekiah's Tunnel, built eight hundred years before.

The elderly blind man finished bathing and stepped out of the pool. He looked directly at Jesus and said, "Thank you. I have not been able to see since birth. I am truly grateful, Master."

"Go, my friend and tell others that God Almighty has healed you." Jesus smiled. All the spectators and bathers were amazed at the healing of the blind man. The old man threw on his robe over his wet loincloth and left.

All the disciples except for the women members, stripped off their robes leaving only their loincloths on. Like happy children playing, they all entered the Pool of Siloam. It was a rectangular shaped pool with plenty of room for them to bathe in.

Mary Magdalene and Sarah stepped into the water up to their knees letting the bottom of their robes get wet. Everyone enjoyed the soothing water. A few of the men laughed as they relaxed in this ancient pool.

Finally, one by one, each disciple along with Jesus and his brother Judah, stepped out of the pool just below the stone columns that surrounded one side of this popular bathing pool. The slight warmth of the day helped them to dry off just a bit. They all threw their robes back on over their still damp loincloths. Mary and Sarah sat beside the pool with their feet still in the water.

It was a pleasant time for all of them as the men gathered near the pool with the towering columns just above.

"Heal me too, Master Jesus," beseeched a middle age man who walked painfully with a crutch under his left armpit. He hobbled forward and stood before Jesus. Judah leaned against a pillar as he watched the event unfold.

Jesus opened up his arms and then placed them onto the shoulders of the man. The crippled man moaned as he was worked on. Suddenly, he stood straighter and smiled as relief from the crippling pain left his body.

"Throw away your crutch!" commanded Jesus. "Go forth and walk freely now on. Let everyone know that your faith in the healing power of the one true God has freed you."

The man that was no longer crippled thanked the Master Teacher and then threw away his crutch, and walked away from the pool. The few people left in the pool area, besides the disciples, were amazed and murmured to each other.

The crowd that greeted them during the triumphal entry into Jerusalem had diminished greatly. All the disciples, along with Jesus and Judah, decided to leave the city, and return to the area beside the home of Lazarus on the Mount of Olives. Later on, a few of the disciples would retire to the establishment of Nicodemus which was called the Upper Room. It was within the city walls and a short distance from the Mount of Olives.

As they meandered through the streets, Judah the twin brother mentioned something that was troubling him deeply. "Brother, I do not like what the money changers are doing in the court of the great temple. They are all thieves who take advantage of the devout worshippers. I want to do something about it but do not know what would work best."

His brother stopped in his tracks and turned to look at his twin. "Let it be, Judah. I suspect we already have upset the high priests and some other members of the Great Sanhedrin. If we do anything, it will put all of us in grave danger, not just me." He put his hand on his brother's shoulder, and then turned and continued walking through the narrow streets.

Jesus had a bad feeling about Judah's comments. Both he and his mother had constantly tried to keep Judah's temper in check through the years. Even though his twin had gotten better and more relaxed over time, his temper did erupt on occasion.

The Master Teacher pushed his worries away and kept walking through the old streets. It felt like a maze here. Soon, they left the city and headed back to the Mount of Olives.

Chapter Nineteen

"Judas, let us go for a walk together. I need to talk with you," said Jesus as he beckoned for his disciple to join him. It was a cool evening so both of them threw their cloaks on over their robes.

They sauntered slowly along the top of the Mount of Olives, past several old olive trees and a few oak trees. There was a moon that was almost full shining down upon the Kidron Valley below.

Both Judas and Jesus continued until they reached the top of the ancient stairway that led into the Garden of Gethsemane. This was the same stairs that Jesus had used several times to gain access to the garden where he taught Joseph of Arimathea and other private students. Even Claudia, the wife of Pontius Pilatus had come here for a few private instructions.

They made their way carefully down the old stairway. Once in the garden, they both sat down on soft grass under very old olive trees. There were many flowers growing here which gave the place a feeling of peace and serenity. Jesus loved being able to teach here in privacy. The ancient stairway allowed him to enter this lovely place unnoticed. This garden was one of the favourite places for Jesus to teach his secret students. It offered quietude and solitude. He even prayed and meditated here on occasion.

"I have very important things to discuss with you, Judas." Jesus ran his hands through his long hair and looked around the garden. "I have great trust in you and know that you will do as I ask. My request is very special and only you can make it so."

Judas sat beside him and looked up at the almost full moon above. It was very peaceful here. He felt relaxed and at peace in this garden as he waited for Jesus to continue.

"Since I was a child, I have had visions of future events, some of them are hundreds of years ahead. Many of these visions come true in their own way. One of these visions keeps repeating itself." He took in a deep breath, held it for a few second, then released it and kept talking, "I have seen a large religion based on me, my healings and my teachings. In it, I am made into a God, something I am not. I am merely a man. I saw countless thousands of people worshipping me. Thousands of buildings had been erected in my name.

This is something I do not want but feel powerless to do anything about."

"Why would you have a problem with that?" Judas Iscariot asked as he scratched his black beard and gazed at the flowers and trees. "You want to be well known and let what you teach get into the public. The healing that you do and taught us to do, is very important. Maybe your vision is the way it needs to unfold."

"No. No! I want my message and teachings out there for the masses but not in this manner." Jesus looked exasperated. He glanced up at the beautiful night sky. It was so peaceful here. How could anyone have a problem when they sat and meditated in this garden?

"Judas, since I was a child I received these types of prophetic visions. I do believe it is a gift from God. My latest vision has been a bit disturbing. I keep seeing my arrest and eventual crucifixion. But something seems odd about it. My vision later shows me alive and healthy with my wife beside me. I am lecturing to my disciples and feel a sadness I cannot explain intermingled with great hope for the future of humankind.

I am also concerned for you. For some reason, you are not there. I fear that you are dead and so is my twin brother Judah Thomas.

"Hopefully, this part of the vision does not come true." He sighed deeply, and looked at the old olive trees and the flowers that grew amongst them.

"You are a great prophet as well as a powerful healer and spiritual teacher. We must trust in God and let the future unfold as it should." Judas Iscariot with his dark hair and beard glanced at his teacher. The slight breeze blowing through the

Garden of Gethsemane felt wonderful. He could almost imagine the old olive presses that stood here many years ago. After all, Gethsemane was the Aramaic name for olive presses.

They sat in silence for a moment, and enjoyed the scenery and the peace within this special garden. This, along with the Sea of Galilee, was one of Jesus's favourite spots. A soul could be recharged here amongst the ancient olive trees.

Finally, Jesus spoke, "I need you to do something important for me, my friend. I want you to go to Caiaphas, the High Priest and report me to him. In other words, betray me to him. You must ask to be paid thirty pieces of silver for the information. Then, make arrangements to go back to him later so that you can lead his temple guards to where I will be. The first time you visit him, tell him that you will come back with my whereabouts. On the second visit, as mentioned, you can direct his guards to where I will be. This will be the Garden of Gethsemane where we now sit.

"It is imperative that you demand the thirty pieces of silver as a payment for turning me in. Thirty is the number that is written about in certain books of the bible in ancient times. The prophet Zechariah was paid thirty pieces of silver for working as a shepherd. On another occasion, thirty pieces of silver was the payment given when a slave died. This sum of money is mentioned in the book of Jeremiah too. The number thirty makes sense.

Besides, thirty pieces of silver for betraying me to Caiaphas is equivalent to about six months income for a labourer. This amount should seem fair to the High Priest.

I need you to go this evening to the house of Caiaphas. Then, tomorrow you will make your second visit to him just after we have our supper at the Upper Room of Nicodemus's house in Jerusalem." Jesus stopped talking and waited for Judas to respond.

"What! Are you mad?" Judas was stunned by the strange requests. "No. I will not do it. It is madness and extremely dangerous."

The Master Teacher raised his hand and said, "Listen. Listen to me, my loyal friend. It is not madness. It is part of my destiny. It is imperative that this be done. If you follow my instructions, our movement will grow and it will help millions worldwide."

Judas calmed down and let his anger diminish. He thought about this request by his teacher. He finally nodded his head and said, "Very well. I will follow your request. I will go to the house of Caiaphas, and report your whereabouts to him and lead his men to you. Jesus, I hope you know what you are doing. Do you?"

His teacher looked at him with compassion in his eyes. He knew Judas would understand his reasons and would do his bidding. "Yes. I know exactly what I am doing. Do you agree to help me?" He needed to be certain that Judas would do his bidding. Judas nodded slowly.

"Good. After we gather for our communal supper at the Upper Room, just before the meal is finished, I want you to go to the house of Caiaphas, the High Priest, with the purpose of leading his men to me in the Garden of Gethsemane. This is as I have requested. Tell him that you will identify me with a kiss on the cheek. Then, his temple guards can arrest me."

Jesus gathered his thoughts and then leaned forward with both hands. "Judas, shut your eyes, take a deep breath in and let the vision come to you."

The Master Teacher placed his hands on top of Judas Iscariot's head and asked for energy from above to enter into the head of his student.

Suddenly, the disciple started to receive vivid visions of future events. He saw the same things that Jesus had seen earlier. Thousands of buildings had been built in the name of Jesus. Millions of people worshipped him in a new religion that had grown. The Roman Empire accepted the teachings of Jesus as a religion of the people. As the scenes unfolded, Judas saw people fighting and dying in the name of Jesus. It frightened him. Many people from different parts of the world gathered in large masses in his name.

Many terrible events unfolded due to this newly formed religion. People were tortured and burnt alive on stakes if they did not follow the beliefs demanded by leaders of the church that formed around this religion.

The scene quickly changed to two male angels bathed in white light gazing at him with love. He could feel this incredible joy as he lay there with his eyes shut. The love and peace was almost indescribable. In his head, he heard the angels say, "You must do this. It is important."

Finally, the visions stopped, Jesus removed his hands from the top of Judas's head. The loyal disciple collapsed on the ground. It took a few moments before Judas opened his eyes. Jesus was looking down at him with concern. "Are you alright, my friend?"

"Yeah." Judas shook his head and then sat up. "Now I understand why you want me to do this. If not, the movement will not expand and become universal. It is very important that you and I do this."

"Exactly," Jesus beamed. "This action will ensure that the movement will continue forward for a long time. We will touch the hearts and souls of millions of people over the centuries.

This evening, I would like you to go to the home of Caiaphas and ask for thirty pieces of silver. In exchange, you will offer to take his men to arrest me the next evening once you are certain of the location."

Judas Iscariot nodded his head in understanding. The task would be daunting for him but he knew how vital it was for the movement.

 "I want to change the subject now and talk about something on a spiritual level. You have often heard me talk about heaven in my sermons to our followers," Jesus spoke with passion and played with his beard unconsciously. "Heaven consists of several levels or fields. This explanation of heaven is not known to you. I think it is best that we discuss it now. Everything is based on vibrations. Our earth vibrates at a certain frequency or energy level. The levels of heaven vibrate at much higher frequencies. There are twelve levels and each one vibrates at a higher level than the one before. In other words, the first level or field exists at a certain vibration or energy level. The second level is even higher and so on. In heaven, there are healing temples, teaching temples, gardens and much more. Each level contains its own characteristics.

For instance, the first level contains beautiful healing gardens along with healing hospitals. This is where the souls of newly departed humans go initially.

The second level or field contains loved ones whom have passed over. They gather here and enjoy each other's company. This happens after they move from the first level. At this point, the soul is healed, and ready to rest and receive spiritual lessons. You will be able to visit the higher levels including the eleventh and twelve levels. Your soul will vibrate to extremely high energy and visit these amazing places. It is here that the true essence of God and healing energy exists.

Finally, when your soul is ready, you will have a meeting with spiritual elders. Together, all of you will find the perfect arrangement for your next incarnation on earth. The place of birth, your new parents and even your sex will be decided prior to returning to earth. As a little soul, you will enter the womb of your soon to be mother. You will be born as a new baby. You will live, die and eventually return home to heaven. This is done for your greatest spiritual growth.

As you are aware through earlier sermons, your eternal soul will incarnate over and over until you become spiritually enlightened. As an enlightened soul, you will return to the heavenly fields and remain there.

Heaven is very beautiful and is our true home. Breaking the karmic pattern of birth, death and re-birth is the goal for all of us," Jesus finished speaking, took in a few deep breaths and looked around at the peaceful garden.

"Your soul will gain great growth for what you are about to do, Judas. Do not worry what others may think. I will tell the disciples that you are doing my bidding." The Teacher smiled and put his hand on his loyal disciple's shoulder. "I think it is time to head back to the home of Lazarus. This evening you have a date with destiny."

Chapter Twenty

"Lord Caiaphas, there is a man here that wishes to speak with you. He says his name is Judas Iscariot and he is a follower of Jesus," Simon, the chief spy for the High Priest announced.

"Bring him here, Simon," commanded Caiaphas. "I am curious to hear what he has to say."

Judas was impressed by the size and grandeur of the home of the High Priest. It was a small palace with high walls, an outer courtyard and an inner one equipped with a water fountain. Exotic potted plants were positioned throughout along with some minor garden areas.

Minor priests and several temple guards could be seen in hallways, and outside the doors that led into private rooms. Expensive furniture filled areas of Caiaphas's opulent palace. There were several other courts within the complex.

Joseph Caiaphas resided here in splendour. Many servants, including Simon the spy, did his bidding. As a very rich man, he paid his helpers well.

Judas walked through the home and entered a smaller court area. Caiaphas stood there looking at him with curiosity. Beside him stood his father-in-law, Annas.

Annas was the previous Chief High Priest in Jerusalem. He was tall and slender with thinning white hair. Annas was a very rich man. He still held great influence on the temple and the Sanhedrin.

"You wanted to see me, Judas Iscariot?" asked Caiaphas. He was quite interested in hearing the answer.

The disciple of Jesus took a moment to gather his thoughts. He said, "As a trusted follower of Jesus the Master Teacher, I have information that can help you.

I know you have an intense dislike of him and would love to see him silenced. I can provide the solution to your problem.

For thirty pieces of silver in Tyrian shekels, I will provide the exact location where Jesus will be tomorrow evening."

"Why would you betray Jesus? You are one of his followers," asked Caiaphas with puzzlement.

Judas answered with a believable lie, "I have been associated with the Zealots in Galilee. They are waiting for a leader to free us from the yoke of the Romans. The Zealots will not attack the Romans as it would be an end to all of them. They do not have the power and military might to do so. They are realistic. They believe a great leader will arise and lead them to victory with the help of God.

I thought Jesus would be that leader and lead us to a victory over the Romans. Unfortunately, he is not that person. He practices peace and compassion to all including our enemies. For that reason, I have decided to turn him in to you. I am also a greedy man and would like to profit in this venture. The silver is about a half year's salary and would help me."

The Chief High Priest and his father-in-law, Annas gazed at him intently. It was a moment before Caiaphas spoke, "Fine. This makes perfect sense to me. Your request is reasonable. I will be right back." A few moments later, Caiaphas returned and handed Judas a leather bag. The coins clinked inside.

Annas said in a thoughtful manner, "I want to question this Jesus. I would like to do that first, Caiaphas."

The High Priest nodded his head slowly in agreement. "It is agreed. We will expect you here tomorrow with the whereabouts of Jesus. You will lead my temple guards to his location then."

"Yes. I will guide them tomorrow evening. I will kiss Jesus on the cheek to identify him." Judas hefted the leather bag full of coins in his right hand. The weight felt right.

Caiaphas smiled and looked at his chief spy, Simon. "You will accompany my guards tomorrow evening when they arrest the rabble rouser Jesus."

The chief spy was happy about this. He would receive more money from the High Priest soon.

"You have served me well by bringing me reports about Jesus and his disciples. I especially appreciated you telling me about him entering Jerusalem on a donkey. I hope to use these events against him," Caiaphas continued.

He and his father-in-law watched Judas Iscariot leave the courtyard, and head out of the complex.

Once outside, Judas leaned against a wall and made sure nobody was nearby. He untied the leather bag and put some of the silver coins into his palm. The coins were as he had requested, Tyrian shekels. The pagan deity Herakles was on the obverse and an eagle graced the reverse of the coins.

Although pagan images were not to be used in the Holy Temple, the priests ignored this rule or commandment. Tyrian shekels contained high quality of silver and therefore, were welcomed by the authorities of the Temple. These coins were in active circulation here in Jerusalem and area.

He placed the coins back into the leather bag and shoved it into the recesses of his robe. With a sense of relief mingled with some guilt, Judas left the city proper and went back to the home of Lazarus on the Mount of Olives.

That evening, he and Jesus sat on the ground looking out over Jerusalem across the Kedron valley. It was pleasant and a slight wind blew across their faces. The moon overhead was nearly full.

"It is all arranged, Jesus. I will return to the house of Caiaphas at this time and then lead his temple guards to your location. I will kiss you on the cheek to identify you," Judas explained with apprehension in his heart.

"Good. I will be found in the Garden of Gethsemane tomorrow evening at this time. It is my favourite spot to visit when I come here. Some of the disciples, my brother, my wife and my mother Mary will be there. They all believe we are gathering there to meditate and pray. No one suspects you or me of planning anything this dangerous. It will be under the cover of darkness in a secluded spot where I will be found away from the main entrance." Jesus took a deep breath, enjoyed the smells of the evening, released his breath slowly, and said, "Thank you, Judas. You have done more than you will ever know."

The almost full moon peaked out from behind the clouds like a white specter watching the scene below. It created a feeling of peace here. Jesus felt it was best to enjoy this special moment for who truly knew what tomorrow would bring.

Chapter Twenty-One

"My house shall be called a house of prayer. But you have made it into a den of robbers," screamed Judah Thomas. He shoved, slapped and pushed the moneylenders out of the temple. He overturned their tables as well. Coins, mostly silver, flew onto the stone floor.

His anger unleashed, he pushed the rest of the moneylenders out of the area. The benches of those selling doves were overturned also. Many of them ran in fear out of the Holy Temple.

Annas, the former High Priest, gazed down at the chaotic scene before him. He could not believe his eyes. As far as he was concerned, a big child had just had a bad temper tantrum. Anger built inside him. Jesus, the troublemaker was costing him a lot of money. He could not wait to have this man in his custody soon.

The noise and commotion drew his son-in-law Caiaphas out of the interior to stand beside him. The Chief High Priest's eyes went wide as he observed the destructive scene below.

"That bastard will be in our hands tonight. He will pay for this too," promised Caiaphas as he folded his hands together in front of him. "We do not need to arrest him now in the courtyard. That would create a small riot. Tonight will be much easier."

"Yes. He has cost me a great deal of money today. He will answer for it and much more." The older man played with his white beard. Annas loved his family but loved wealth and power almost as much. He was a petty vindictive man who did not forgive his enemies, even if it was years after the event. He had financially destroyed anyone who got in his way. A vein in his forehead throbbed.

Both men thought of Jesus as a threat to their esteemed positions and authority. They did not want to upset their Roman masters and lose their power. Neither knew it was Judah Thomas, the twin brother of Jesus who had overturned the tables below, and drove out the moneylenders and sellers of doves. This evening would prove very interesting.

Jesus leaned against a massive pillar and watched the scene transpire. "I always knew Judah's temper would cause trouble."

He announced to all the group, "Simon, Andrew, see if you can bring him back. Then we can leave the temple before the temple guards show up, or worse, Roman soldiers." He nodded at the brothers.

It took a bit of work but eventually they brought Judah back to where Jesus and the others were gathered. The twin brother of Jesus was starting to calm down. His red face was getting lighter as he stood in front of his brother breathing heavily. "Well, are you going to chastise me, brother?"

"Why, bother? You would not listen anyway," replied Jesus. "We must leave here at once. If we do not, we could all be arrested."

As an afterthought, he said, "Both our mother and I have always warned you about your bad temper. I hope you have not put all our lives in peril."

Judah now looked sheepish. He turned and left the temple complex along with everyone else. Simon and Andrew were very annoyed with him for causing trouble, and drawing unnecessary attention to them.

Simon who had a fiery temper himself, walked beside Judah. "I am the one who has to watch my temper. I was able to restrain myself. Too bad you could not do the same. Let us pray that you did not put our lives in danger with your stupid actions." He stormed ahead of Judah and kept walking briskly through the streets of Jerusalem.

Two of the other disciples, Bartholomew and Matthew went to the Upper Room of the home of Nicodemus. The rest continued until they reached the area near the dwelling of Lazarus in Bethany. All were worried about a possible retaliation from the High Priest Caiaphas and his fellow priests associated with the Sanhedrin.

This august body of men was the religious and political authority of Jerusalem and the surrounding area. These men answered directly to their Roman masters on all matters concerning law and governance. The Romans left them on a loose leash for the moment.

Jesus sat on the side of the Mount of Olives and reflected on everything. This evening would be a monumental one for him and everyone he cared about. He did not look forward to the upcoming evening.

Chapter Twenty-Two

That evening by twos and threes like thieves in the night, all members of the group ventured to the Upper Room in Jerusalem. Stealth and secrecy was vital.

Andrew and his red headed brother Simon leaned against a wall, and peered around the corner at the home of Nicodemus where the Upper Room was located. The street in front was all clear so they walked quickly across the street, through the front door and into the dwelling. There was a set of stone steps that led up to the Upper Room. All the disciples including the female members had gathered for suppers here many times in the past.

The smells of cooked food greeted their nostrils. The different aromas were wonderful. Garlic, fish and baked bread smells filled the room.

With the arrival of Andrew and Simon, all members of the spiritual group were present. Mary Magdalene, Martha of Bethany and Ann, a young follower, were busy setting the low tables. Some of the male disciples started putting dishes of food onto other tables that were positioned in front of three couches. These couches were arranged in a U shape. Everyone would recline on these comfortable couches and eat their delicious supper in the same manner that the Romans did at meals. Every cushion was placed alongside these couches so additional people could sit here and eat too.

The low tables covered with dishes and containers were semi-arranged in a rough circle. Several disciples including Matthew the former tax collector and John the youngest one, were gathered about the large room. Rugs and many cushions were scattered about.

Also among the group in this large room were James, the son of Zebedee, Phillip of Bethsaida, Thomas, Bartholomew,

James, son of Alphaeus also called James the Lesser, Simon the Zealot, Thaddaeus-Judas, brother of Matthew the tax collector and Judas Iscariot.

Judah Thomas and his mother Mary were among the many present in the Upper Room as well. It was interesting to note that most of the main twelve disciples came from Capernaum and nearby Bethsaida.

Mary Magdalene finished setting down plates onto the many tables that were arranged in front of the couches and looked about the room at all gathered there. She was proud of her husband and all of his followers. Amazing deeds had been performed by Jesus, his brother Judah and some of the disciples. The spiritual message was getting out there.

A cook and two helpers had been hired to prepare the supper, and serve the food that evening. Nobody knew this would be the last supper here in the Upper Room. In the past, countless suppers had been eaten here by all the disciples.

Fish, lamb, beans, vegetables, fruits, and fine red wine adorned all the low tables set before and beside the three main reclining couches.

Seeing that, Jesus went to the middle couch and sat down putting a cushion behind his back. He motioned everyone to join him. His lovely wife, Mary sat down beside him on his right hand side. The twelve main disciples found spots to recline on the couches and used cushions for support as well. His mother Mary and his twin brother Judah Thomas sat near the end of the couch positioned on the right of the middle one. Martha of Bethany, who was attracted to Judah, sat beside him. Other followers sat on cushions that were on the rug covered floor.

The Master Teacher looked about the room at all gathered here. The cook's helpers lighted oil lamps that were conveniently placed throughout the Upper Room. The smell of food including the freshly baked bread, and the lights gave the room a warm and inviting feeling.

Jesus poured the fine red wine into a wooden cup. Everyone followed his example. Several jugs had been placed upon the low tables in front making it easy for all to reach and pour the red liquid into their cups.

Once everyone had poured a cup, Jesus began to speak, "I am following in the tradition of the Essenes this evening. Our supper will be a ritual for all of us.

The Essenes have a Holy Communion or Eucharist where bread and red wine are used as symbols; bread represents the body, and red wine symbolizes the blood.

I have never done this with most of you before. Only a few of you have shared in this ritual with me in the past. My brother Judah, my mother Mary and my beloved wife, Mary Magdalene have participated in this special ceremony with me. Since this will be our last supper here, I thought it was appropriate. This ceremony will be in conjunction with the Passover. This way we can celebrate both events at the very same time. I…"

"What are you talking about?" roared Simon as he slammed his fist onto the wooden table in front of him. Luckily, nothing on it fell over. "We have come here for three years now. Why the end to this tradition we began?"

"Simon, I must…"

The red bearded disciple interrupted Jesus again, "This does not make sense." His flushed, and angry face only made his beard and hair look like they were on fire.

"Let me finish, my friend. My arrest and eventual death is very near. We must have this final supper together with the Essene ritual this evening. My time on earth is coming to an end. Many of you will continue my work and make the movement grow."

He could hear the mumbling and unhappy murmurs as he gazed about the large upper chamber. "Before I forget, I want to thank John and Simon for arranging everything this evening." He nodded at both of these important disciples. Simon no longer looked like he was on fire.

All present became silent for a brief moment as they digested the sad announcement their spiritual leader had just made.

Jesus's brother stood up then and said, "What nonsense is this? Are you in danger because of my actions in the Holy Temple when I overturned the moneychanger tables? If so, I am truly sorry."

"No. No. Sit down, my brother. You are all aware of my gift of prophecy. I have had several visions in the last few months showing my arrest and crucifixion. A close member of our group will betray me as per my wishes. It is meant to be."

Simon the former fisherman stood up again. "I will protect you. I will not let anyone arrest you." His brown eyes blazed with passion.

The Master Teacher rose to his feet. "My friend, you will deny me after I have been arrested. In fact, when asked by people, you will deny ever knowing me. This will happen three times before the cock crows by early morning."

Simon was stunned by this remark. He looked hurt.

"I know that you would protect me with your life. Everyone here would. But I have powerful enemies and you cannot stand against them. I admire your devotion and courage trying to protect me from arrest. But once I have been arrested, Simon, you will do the very strange thing I have just mentioned. Again, you will deny me three times to strangers that recognize you as one of my disciples."

Jesus lifted his hands to quiet and calm everyone down. "Let us eat our supper now." He tore off a piece of unleavened bread and passed the basket to his lovely wife on his right. She ripped off a piece of bread and passed the basket along. Once everyone had bread, Jesus spoke again, "Now. Let us begin. This bread represents my body. Eat this in my memory."

He quickly ate the bread and so did everyone else. He reached forward and grabbed his cup of red wine. He said, "This is my blood. Drink this in my memory." He greedily drank most of the fine red wine from his wooden cup. It was a very, expensive Setine wine that Joseph of Arimathea had imported from Italy originally. All the others gathered on the three main couches drank their wine. Two other couches were positioned in the room with people reclining on them too. Everyone here drank their red wine at the same time.

Jesus then emptied his cup and filled it again with the delicious red liquid that was on a container in front of him. He quickly gulped the wine down.

Soon, he and everyone were partaking of the lamb, fish, beans, and other food. A few people started to laugh as the mood became lighter. There was a somber feeling in the air but the wine and delicious meal helped to make it feel better.

Mary Magdalene reclined beside her husband on the rug covered floor. She noticed that Martha of Bethany and Judah Thomas were leaning close to each other in quiet conversation. She felt happy that Martha showed attention to her brother-in-law. Judah deserved happiness and love in his life too.

The expensive wine flowed as the disciples reclined on rugs and cushions. The clay containers were getting lighter as each person reached for more wine. The meal and celebration continued for close to an hour. Once everyone had their fill of food and wine, they all relaxed. The talking became less as they reclined on the couches.

Judas glanced about the Upper Room and contemplated about what he was to do soon. Fear and apprehension gripped his heart. He thought, *Do I have the strength to go through with this dangerous plan?* He kept watching Jesus who was in the middle of the semi-circle of disciples reclining on the couches. Cushions were strewn everywhere. Empty dishes and dirty plates sat on the low tables before them. The cook and his female helpers hired for this supper gathering started to pick up the dirty dishes.

Jesus and Judas looked across the room at each other at the same time. The Master Teacher nodded his head slowly. Judas took the sign, stood up and headed towards the stairs leading down to the door on the main level.

Simon was like a hawk. He watched with suspicious eyes as his fellow disciple left the room. He asked, "Where is Judas going? Why is he leaving us?"

"He is going to do my bidding, Simon," Jesus replied quickly. He then announced, "We will leave for the Garden of Gethsemane after supper."

The former fisherman scratched the top of his fiery red head, and gave the back of Judas a look that was full of anger and mistrust.

Judah sat up from his reclining position and also watched as Judas left the room. He knew something important was up. His brother and Judas had been in many private discussions over the last few days. His mother Mary reclining on his left hand side sat up too. She had observed the exchange between Jesus and Judas.

Eventually, all the participants went back to eating some more food and drinking. The red wine flowed easily. As everyone became fuller, the room grew quieter. That was when Jesus announced, "Let us head to the Garden of Gethsemane now. I wish to meditate and pray in this special place."

The Upper Room cleared quickly as all headed out.

Chapter Twenty-Three

"I am going to meditate and pray over there," Jesus proclaimed and then pointed at the ground made of grey rock nearby. The rocky area was about five feet wide and ten feet long. Dirt and grass surrounded this area. A nearly full moon shone down on the scene.

"Brother, keep a watchful eye out. Make sure everyone does the same." Jesus looked at his twin brother. He then walked over to the rocky ground and knelt in front of the hard surface.

It was peaceful here in the Garden of Gethsemane. A slight breeze stirred the leaves of the olive and oak trees. The moonlight created a magical feeling.

All the disciples including the women moved into small groups of four in the garden. They were spread out amongst the olive and oak trees.

Judah leaned against a gnarled olive tree. He observed his brother kneeling in deep meditation in front of the rocky ground. At one point, Jesus lifted his head up. Judah shook his own head. He could not believe what he saw. Did drops of red blood run down the face of Jesus?

The mystical moonlight shone down on the Master Teacher and then a bright white light completely surrounded him. The light glowed and pulsed around the head of Jesus, and also lit up his white robe.

Judah was mesmerized by the amazing event. He had never seen the aura this pronounced around his twin brother. This lamination bathed the Master Teacher for several moments. Then it vanished as if it was never there.

Soon, a white mist started floating in the garden like a fog. Judah felt very sleepy as this heavenly mist floated throughout the area and covered the trees. He forced himself to stay awake.

He noticed that Simon, Andrew and Matthew were asleep on the ground nearby.

Judah started to receive vivid visions of what heaven looked like. It was beautiful beyond description. Intense peace filled his heart as he watched the scenes unfold within his head. Then the visions were gone.

He caught a movement out of the corner of his eye. His mother Mary and his sister-in-law Mary Magdalene appeared from behind a group of trees. They approached him. Both ladies were yawning and shaking their heads in order to ward off sleepiness.

"We have something wonderful to tell you, Judah," exclaimed his mother Mary. "Mary may be pregnant. We have to tell your brother Jesus too."

The two Marys smiled at Judah and each gave him a hug. He could feel their joy.

Jesus started to pray fervently. He asked for the strength to endure the upcoming event. "Lord, give me the courage to face my fate. Allow me to be strong." Then he rose from his knees and glanced quickly at the beautiful moon. He turned, and walked towards his wife, mother and brother who were gathered nearby.

Mary Magdalene ran to him and hugged him fiercely. "Husband, I have wonderful news. I believe I am pregnant."

Jesus held on to his wife for a moment longer. This news changed everything. "Are you sure, my love?"

"Yes, a woman knows these things. Our child needs a father. I need you to be there. Whatever you have planned must change now."

They broke their loving embrace and Jesus said, "Of course, you are right. I need to survive and spend my life with you."

He walked briskly over to where the three disciples were sleeping close to each other on the ground. He yelled, "Wake up. Wake up, now."

Simon, Andrew and Matthew stirred, and opened their eyes. They sat up and then each one rose slowly to their feet.

Jesus admonished them sternly, "I asked you to keep a watchful vigilance while I meditated and prayed. Instead, you all fell asleep."

129

Judah Thomas put a hand gently on his brother's shoulder. "Do not be too harsh with them. The power of heaven manifested here this evening was too much for them to handle. The Divine Energy of the Creator came down and affected everyone."

Jesus nodded his head in understanding. He asked Simon, his brother Andrew and Matthew to move closer to the front entrance of the garden. He needed them to watch out for the guards that Judas Iscariot would be bringing shortly.

Just as the three disciples moved forward to join the other disciples, a familiar sound could be heard; the marching feet of soldiers or temple guards approaching the garden. When you lived in this land, the sound of marching feet was known to all.

Simon yelled back at them, "I see temple guards coming towards us along with a quaternion of Roman soldiers behind them. There are two other figures amongst them. One I do not recognise. I do not believe it. The other is Judas!"

Andrew, his brother bellowed, "Run, Jesus, run. Take the ancient stairs up to the top of the mount. The stairs cannot be seen from here. We will try to block them." Fear gripped him as he watched the temple guards and the four Roman soldiers getting closer.

"Quick, hurry. Go," Judah commanded as he pushed his brother and Mary Magdalene back towards where the ancient stairs were located.

His mother Mary helped him too. Between the two of them, Jesus and his wife had enough encouragement to escape the Garden of Gethsemane. They ran to the base of the ancient steps and started to climb them. The nearly full moon provided enough light to allow them to climb quickly.

Mother Mary watched the two of them hurry up the stairs. She could feel her heart beating hard inside. She truly feared for her son's life.

As Jesus and Mary made it halfway up the ancient steps, they could hear angry yells, and metallic clangs from the garden. They worked their way to the top and then continued running along the uneven ground towards Bethany. The noises below were harder to hear. Eventually, the sounds disappeared.

Judas Iscariot cautiously opened the small, ornamental gate that led into the Garden of Gethsemane. When it creaked, the sound seemed to fill the very air.

As he, the chief spy Simon and the six temple guards stepped into the garden, several disciples appeared from behind trees, and started to surround them. The four Roman soldiers, the quaternion, filled in behind. Their hands were on their hilts of their sheathed swords. One of them removed his sword and banged it against the sheath to let everyone know they meant business.

Judas looked about at the menacing disciples until he spotted Jesus standing just back from the rest of them. He stepped forward quickly and embraced the man he thought was Jesus. He kissed the teacher on his cheek. This was the sign that the guards needed to identify and arrest Jesus the troublemaker.

As two temple guards reached out for the man they assumed was Jesus the prophet, Simon the disciple screamed in anger, "No, you bastards. Leave him alone." He pulled out a knife that was hidden in his robes. He rushed forward and started to slice off the left ear of one of these temple guards. The other guards started to unsheathe their swords from their scabbards. The loud sound of metal could be heard by everyone in the previously quiet garden.

The unlucky guard screamed in agony and reached his hand up to his bleeding ear.

"No. No," yelled Judah Thomas as he pushed through the disciples. He took his right hand and put it over the bleeding ear of the temple guard. "Put your knife away, Simon."

The four Roman soldiers along with the rest of the temple guards had all unsheathed their swords. They were ready to attack the followers of Jesus if need be.

"There is great heat coming from your hand," the wounded guard announced. A look of bewilderment filled his eyes.

Soon, a bright light shone around the right hand of Judah as he held it against the bleeding ear. The intense light grew until it completely covered the hand and most of the guard's head. The bleeding stopped. It took a few more seconds and then the mysterious light disappeared.

131

The guard put his hand back up to his ear. The ear had completely healed, only dry blood existed. He was amazed at the miraculous healing.

All who witnessed this event were stunned. A few murmurs were heard amongst the disciples and guards. The Roman soldiers also amazed by this display of healing still kept their swords at the ready. Superstition ran high among them. Fear filled them.

Judas Iscariot had stepped back after kissing Judah on the cheek. Another guard took over for the guard that had been attacked. He and a fellow guard walked towards their prisoner.

"You betray me with a kiss, Judas?" asked Judah, the brother of Jesus.

When Judah turned slightly towards Judas Iscariot, the moon light caught his face clearly. Judas immediately noticed that the eyes of the man before him were brown and not blue. He knew right away that they were about to arrest the wrong man. All he could do was keep his mouth shut.

These two guards moved to Judah whom they believed was Jesus the troublemaker and grabbed both of his arms. One of the guards thrust the arms behind Judah's back while the second tied leather straps together around his wrists. Thus restrained all the guards including the one with the healed ear, surrounded Judah Thomas.

The guards turned with Judah within their ranks and headed out the gate towards Jerusalem. The Roman quaternion spread out slightly and eyed the disciples warily.

Fearing their own imminent arrests, the disciples of Jesus started to flee in several directions. Like rats abandoning a sinking ship, the disciples, including the female ones, fled the Garden of Gethsemane. The olive trees and other trees hid their escape. Several of them even went up the ancient steps at the back of the garden.

In moments, all the members of the movement had abandoned the garden. Only the mother of Jesus and Judah remained. The Roman soldiers glanced at her, sheathed their weapons, turned, and followed after the temple guards and their only prisoner.

She looked around her at the now tranquil garden. She was stunned by it all. It was hard to believe that this beautiful garden had been the site where violence and her son's arrest had taken place. Mary raised her face to the lonely moon. Sadness filled her heart. She then walked back to the ancient steps and worked her way up them. She headed to the village of Bethany where she knew Jesus and Mary Magdalene would be.

The nearly full moon bathed the Garden of Gethsemane in a shimmer of mystical light. Peace and beauty had returned to this magical garden.

Chapter Twenty-Four

Annas, the former Chief High Priest, pointed an accusatory finger at the man they thought was Jesus. "Do you deny that you entered Jerusalem on a borrowed donkey and that you claimed to be the Messiah by this very act?"

Behind him, his son-in-law Caiaphas sat on a large stone chair. He looked like a king on his throne as he glared with hatred at the prisoner before them.

The members of the Sanhedrin, the religious and political council of Jerusalem and the surrounding area, stood around the unlucky prisoner in a full circle. There were seventy-one members of this religious council. Normally, the council would meet in the Hall of Hewn Stones. It was built into the north wall of the temple, half inside the sanctuary and half outside, with doors providing access both to the temple and to the outside. But Caiaphas had convened the trial here in his own home. Some of the members sat on stone benches placed throughout the huge room.

"Well, speak, man. Do you claim to be the Messiah?" yelled Annas.

"No. I am not the Messiah. I merely rode a donkey into the city in order to greet the masses. This is what they wanted," Judah Thomas spoke firmly as he answered his accuser.

His hands were still tied behind his back. The wrists felt tight and uncomfortable. He tried to move his bound wrists. It proved painful.

Joseph of Arimathea rose from a stone bench and moved toward Judah, the twin brother of Jesus. As he approached, he immediately noticed brown eyes and not blue ones looking back at him. *Oh my God*, he thought. *They have arrested the wrong man.*

He whispered in Judah's ear, "Where is your brother Jesus?"

"He is safe in Bethany with his pregnant wife Mary," he answered quietly so no one else could hear him.

"I am very happy to hear that Mary is pregnant. Perhaps, that is why he evaded capture by the temple guards and Roman soldiers. Obviously, you decided to take his place."

"Joseph, do not let Caiaphas and his men know they have the wrong man. If they find out, they will try to capture my brother. They would have no problem in trying to talk the Roman authorities into crucifying both of us."

"Of course, I will keep this secret between us, Judah."

Joseph of Arimathea turned toward Annas and Caiaphas, and said, "This trial is illegal. You had no right or authority to arrest Jesus. You sent guards to arrest him furtively in a garden in the middle of the night. Obviously, you do not want the masses to know. They would never let you do this."

He looked about the huge room full of Sanhedrin members, both standing and sitting, in this courtyard of the house of Caiaphas. Several temple guards stood at attention about the large courtyard. Two heavily armed ones stood by the large archway that opened into another smaller courtyard that was at the edge of the home. Torches were lit and positioned in holders on the walls about this massive room.

"My hands and wrists hurt from being tied up behind my back. Do you think you can get them untied for me, Joseph?" asked Judah as he grimaced.

"Of course. I will ask," Joseph of Arimathea spoke compassionately. He stared directly at the Chief High Priest. "Caiaphas, untie Jesus's hands. He does not need to be tied up like a dangerous prisoner. He is not going anywhere."

Caiaphas sitting on his seat like a king on a throne nodded and motioned the temple guards nearby to untie the prisoner.

When his hands were untied Judah, brought them forward and started to rub his sore wrists. He then flexed his hands to let the blood flow back in. He smiled at Joseph for his help.

"Caiaphas and Annas, you have no authority to have Jesus here. This trial is illegal as I already said. You should release him now. He has done nothing wrong." Joseph glared at the High Priest and his father-in-law.

Annas pointed his finger at the rich merchant and said, "Do not tell us what we can or cannot do. We are the authority in Jerusalem. We will do what we want to do with Jesus."

"You have brought him here at midnight to avoid the crowds. If the people knew what you did, they would rise up against you and Annas. Only the Romans possess the power to put a man on trial. You should be ashamed of yourselves," Joseph ranted loudly at the two men.

The Great Sanhedrin consisted of the Pharisees and the Sadducees. Both sects had different philosophies. The Sadducees were more rigid, manipulative and power hungry. The Pharisees were more interested in serving their fellow Jews. These two sects were constantly at odds with each other. Joseph of Arimathea was a prominent Pharisee.

Caiaphas and his father-in-law were clearly Sadducees. However, Joseph of Arimathea held great sway with his own sect of Pharisees.

The High Priest rose from his seat and said, "Jesus is a threat to us and must be dealt with accordingly. He leaves the impression that he is the Messiah come back to earth. He is purported to raise the dead, heal the blind and the lepers. He draws large crowds to him who beg to be healed by him."

"His gifts come from God above," replied Joseph of Arimathea with passion. "He is not the Messiah but a prophet and great healer. You are jealous of him. You are afraid he will control the multitudes of people and take away your power. Free him. Let him go now!"

Several of the Pharisees murmured their agreement. A few even voiced their opinions to let Jesus go.

"Do not tell me what to do, Joseph. I am the Chief High Priest of Jerusalem. I will decide what to do with him," Caiaphas, his face red with anger, answered. He looked about the courtyard at all the people gathered here. The many torches on the walls flickered and cast a strong glow upon the scene.

He took a few steps forward and asked, "Jesus, are you the Messiah? Are you the son of God as many people have claimed?"

"No," replied Judah Thomas. "I am merely a servant of God. I am here to heal and teach the people. It is my sacred duty to tell them all about heaven above. They must know that it is real and very beautiful."

"Enough. I have heard enough. How can you tell the people what heaven looks like? No one has that ability. As a Sadducee, I do not believe in an afterlife. When you are dead, you are dead. We will reconvene before dawn and make a decision about what to do with you."

As he walked from the huge courtyard back to his private quarters, he announced, "We will meet back here in three hours and decide what to do."

Simon, the loyal follower of Jesus sat in the outer courtyard of Caiaphas's estate. A fire burned bright in the fire pit in front of him. He put his hands out to the flames and warmed them. He was chilled and did not know why. Several other men sat or stood around him taking comfort in the warmth of the flickering flames.

Nearby was a large archway that led out to the streets of the city. Two temple guards walked by the wall on either side of the archway. Dawn was fast approaching. A slight light could be seen in the distance.

Simon coughed clearing his throat. A middle aged man sitting across the fire from him looked his way. He looked away and then took a second glance at the red haired Simon. "I know you. You are one of the followers of Jesus the prisoner. I saw you with him several times."

"No. No, I am not a follower. You are mistaken." Simon shook his head back and forth vigorously.

"Yes. Yes, you are. I saw you standing just beside Jesus the other day."

Simon moved away from the fire and turned towards the grand archway that led out onto the streets. Another man watched him pass and pointed an accusing finger at him, "You are a follower of Jesus. I have seen you many times with him."

"No. No, you are mistaken. I do not know Jesus." Simon walked faster towards the archway. As he did, a third man, tall and slender, leaning against the wall on the left side of the archway yelled at him, "I know you. You are a follower of Jesus. You are a member of his group." The accusation rang through this outer courtyard.

"No. No. I am not," screamed Simon the former fisherman as he sped up and exited through the prominent archway. A rooster crowed nearby. The prophecy had come true.

Judah Thomas slept fitfully on the hard stone floor of the courtyard. He used his cloak as a pillow. The Sanhedrin had retired several hours ago. This gave him the opportunity to catch up on some greatly needed sleep.

He woke up slowly as Joseph of Arimathea shook him. "Time to wake up, Judah," whispered the rich merchant. "The council is returning and will be deciding your fate soon. I will do what I can. Unfortunately, my fellow Pharisees do not wield enough power in the Sanhedrin. But I will try."

Judah felt stiff and sore as he sat up. Then he rose to his feet and blinked his bleary eyes. "Joseph, do you know what they are planning?" he asked.

"I am not sure but I think they may turn you over to Pontius Pilatus, the prefect. That would be my guess." Joseph added, "If they do, it might be better for you."

Caiaphas, the High Priest, came into the huge inner courtyard and sat in his customary chair. Annas stood beside him on his right. The rest of the Sanhedrin shuffled in and sat on benches or stood around the prisoner in a semi-circle.

The High Priest stood up and said, "Let us continue with what we started. I am going to ask you once again, Jesus. Are you the Messiah?"

"No. No, I am not. I have told you and Annas that before. I am a teacher and a healer," Judah Thomas announced with an angry voice.

Joseph of Arimathea standing nearby nodded his head in agreement. Many murmured their approval of this answer.

The torchlights still flickered against the walls as the sun rose. Once in a while, they would spurt and crackle. There were a few potted palms placed around the courtyard. The torches cast an eerie light on the plants.

Joseph looked directly at Annas and said in an accusatory manner, "Annas, you illegally tried Jesus last night only because he lost you money when he chased away the moneylenders and dove sellers. Normally, you receive a percentage of the proceeds from these men.

It is greed that drives you and not justice." He turned his attention to the current High Priest. "Caiaphas, it is illegal to try someone at night-time. It is also illegal to put someone on trial during a feast. Jesus was entitled to representation but none was granted him when you both tried and accused him last night," He nodded towards the father-in-law of Caiaphas as he stated this.

He could hear words of encouragement from his fellow members of the Pharisee sect as he spoke. The Sadducees along with their leader the High Priest, protested strongly. Some even hissed at Joseph of Arimathea. The sounds became louder as each side let their emotions out. Most of the Sadducees were gathered around Caiaphas and his father-in-law Annas in a rough semi-circle. Joseph had the Pharisees near him.

Finally, the rich merchant and secret student of Jesus shouted, "If you cannot let this man go free then at least let the Romans decide his fate. Only the Romans have the power to execute anyone. I do not think Pontius Pilatus would be interested in condemning an innocent man just to please you. He is not here to do your bidding, Caiaphas."

The High Priest glared back at the handsome face of Joseph of Arimathea and exclaimed, "Jesus has committed blasphemy. He should be punished for his crime. Perhaps, you are right that only the Romans can execute a prisoner. So, I think I will take your advice and send him to Pilatus. The governor is here in Jerusalem at his official residence in Herod's palace. He is here to maintain order during the Passover. Yes. Let us send Jesus to the prefect."

Annas spoke up, "Send Jesus to Pontius Pilatus." Other Sadducees voiced their agreement with that decision; so did some of the Pharisees. Only Joseph of Arimathea and a few others kept quiet.

Caiaphas the Chief High Priest asked one final question, this time directed at the rich merchant, "Joseph, are you a follower of Jesus the so-called prophet? If so, be very careful in the future."

"Jesus and his family are close friends of mine. Whom I follow or do not follow is none of your concern. I do not appreciate the subtle threat you directed at me. I have many

139

rich and powerful friends, Caiaphas. Keep that in mind." He lifted his chin in defiance and stared harshly at the High Priest.

Two Temple guards bound the hands of Judah Thomas in the front this time. Caiaphas, other priests and minor Temple authorities led the way out of the main courtyard. Others along with the bound prisoner followed behind. Joseph decided not to join them and headed home to catch up on some needed sleep.

When they arrived at the palace of Herod, the group of men waited outside the gates of the Roman prefect's residence. Being Jews, they refused to enter because they thought it would defile them.

In a few moments, the huge gates were thrown open and Romans fell out. Marcus, a centurion, was amongst them. He was tall, stocky and resembled a gladiator with his well-muscled body. He recognized the High Priest and his father-in-law. "Lord Caiaphas, what is all this about? Who is this prisoner?" Marcus glanced at the man with his hands tied in front. The centurion spoke crude Greek with a Syrian accent.

"This is the so-called prophet Jesus from Galilee. We have condemned him for blasphemy. We are turning him over to Pontius Pilatus to execute as we do not have the authority to do so."

Marcus crossed his burly arms and said, "Blasphemy is not our problem. We do not care about such things."

"Yes, I know. However, there are serious reasons why Pontius Pilatus will be interested in trying and executing this trouble-maker."

"Oh! And what would that be?" asked Marcus. He kept his powerful arms folded. A wicked scar could be clearly seen on his right arm.

"He incites actions against Rome and he proclaims himself King of the Jews to his many followers. This is clearly an act of sedition or treason. He also believes himself to be the Messiah that will remove the Roman yoke."

Caiaphas continued, "Jesus proclaimed himself this Messiah when he rode into Jerusalem on a donkey. He attacked the money changers and dove sellers in the court of the Temple. He has a huge following and we fear that he may lead them against us."

"That is not true," yelled Judah Thomas as he heard the lies spoken. A temple guard standing beside him slapped him on the back of the head to shut him up. The prisoner brought his tied hands up towards the back of the head to ease the pain and prevent a second attack.

Marcus, tall and intimidating, uncrossed his muscular arms and said, "We will take the prisoner from you. We will take him to the prefect."

He motioned at two soldiers who grabbed the prisoner roughly by the arms, and hauled and partly dragged him through the gates into the Fortress Antonia. This Fortress had always been a part of King Herod the Great's palace complex. The gates slammed shut on the high priests, temple guards and the Chief High Priest of the Sanhedrin.

Chapter Twenty-Five

Judah Thomas stood before Pontius Pilatus, the prefect of Judea. As the governor of this province, Pilatus held power over the land, and power over life and death. His word was the law of Rome.

The governor of Judea examined the man they called Jesus closely. This prisoner did not look like a threat to Rome or anyone else for that matter. He looked pathetic.

Pontius decided to stand up from his marble throne and step closer to Jesus. He was a tall, slender man of equestrian rank. He possessed a long Roman nose that gave him a handsome, regal look. His hair on his head was starting to thin a bit. He kept it combed forward to hide this fact. He wore a short white tunic. Brown leather boots adorned his feet. Pontius kept a sheathed sword buckled about his waist. A gold necklace decorated his neck. His fingers had several expensive rings on them. He commanded great power and many could feel it emanating from him when they were in his presence.

"Jesus, I need to ask you a few questions." He stroked his clean shaven chin as he thought about what to ask first. "Joseph Caiaphas and his other high priests say you claim to be King of the Jews. Is this claim true? Do you believe yourself to be King of the Jews?"

Judah lifted his brown haired head up and looked directly at Pontius Pilatus. "No, I am not the King of the Jews. Caiaphas makes that claim about me so that I can be tried and convicted of treason. The Sanhedrin illegally convicted me of blasphemy in their trial last night. The Chief High Priest fears and hates me deeply."

Pontius listened intently, and then stepped back and sat down on his marble chair in the praetorium. An inner courtyard was directly below him. He often sentenced criminals here on the terrace or balcony. So, when the masses were gathered below in the courtyard, they could see the power of Rome in operation.

"Hmmm. Caiaphas and the other high priests of the Sanhedrin say that people believe you to be the Messiah. If my memory serves me well, the Messiah is a leader who will remove the Romans and restore Judea to a rule similar to King David's time. Is this true? Well, Jesus speak up."

"No, Governor Pilatus. It is not true. I am merely a spiritual leader, healer and teacher. I provide comfort for human souls and the spiritual needs of my followers. I have no political or military aspirations.

Caiaphas, his father-in-law, Annas and the others speak falsehoods. They simply wish to have you execute me so I no longer interfere in their lives. In fact, Annas wishes me dead because I cost him a great deal of money when I overturned the tables of the moneylenders and dove sellers."

Pilatus laughed heartily upon hearing that. "Good for you. Annas is a very petty and extremely greedy man. I heard that there was an incident in the Temple courtyard." He chuckled a bit more at the thought of what happened.

The governor folded his strong yet slender arms and said, "I do not believe you are guilty of any crimes against Rome. Since you are innocent, I must figure out what to do with you.

Jesus, where are you from? Your Greek is excellent but has a strange accent to it."

"I am from the Galilee. I currently live in Capernaum, and travel in the area to teach the people and heal the sick. As you are aware, many people speak Greek in the Galilee."

"Ah, yes. I have the perfect solution. Herod Antipater also known as Antipas is the Tetrarch of Galilee. He is currently here in Jerusalem to attend your Passover festival. Therefore, I will send you to him. I will leave it up to him to do what he wants with you. Since you seem innocent of any crimes, I doubt that he will harm you."

Pontius Pilatus smiled at his own cleverness. "Oh, I almost forgot to mention this. My wife, Claudia Procula is an admirer of you and your teachings. She would be greatly upset with me if I harmed you."

It was now Judah's turn to smile, "Yes, your wife Claudia is a warm and caring person. I have seen her amongst the female followers. I wish her all the best."

The Prefect slapped his hands together, and the Centurion Marcus and another soldier appeared from behind the archway directly behind them. "Marcus, take this man to Herod Antipater in the other part of the Fortress. But first, I will write a short message to Herod." The centurion slammed his fisted arm over his breastplate in response.

Judah, the man everyone believed to be Jesus, now stood before the Tetrarch of Galilea and Perea. Herod Antipater, the oldest son of King Herod the Great was nicknamed Antipas. The Romans, his family and close friends referred to him by this nickname.

He was of average height and well proportioned. He would have been considered a ruggedly handsome man if it was not for his large nose. His prominent nose made him look like a boxer who had participated in one too many fist fights.

"So, you are the man they call Jesus. I have heard many stories about you. Some say you can heal the sick. Some even say you can raise the dead or walk on water. Well, I would like to see that. Walking on water, really?" Herod laughed at the thought of someone walking on water as if by magic.

With strong hands and nimble fingers, Herod carefully opened the scroll that came from the Roman Governor of Judea. He stretched the document out with his hands and read the short message. "Ah, according to this, Pontius Pilatus thinks that you are innocent. He states that Josephus Caiaphas, the Chief High Priest, fears and hates you. He wants to see you executed."

A silver cup full of red wine sat on a wooden table. The Tetrarch of Galilee rolled up the scroll, put it onto another table and picked up the cup of wine. He drank greedily from it and emptied the contents. He then snapped his fingers, and a young, male servant nearby brought over a small jar and poured more wine into the beautiful silver cup.

The servant then filled another silver cup that Herodias, the wife of Herod, held in her dark skinned hands. She was still a beautiful woman. Her dark features gave her an exotic look. A bit of silver-grey tinged her long black hair. Expensive rings covered every finger of both her hands. A heavy gold necklace ordained her lovely neck. Her ample bosom could almost be seen over the top of her gown.

"Antipas, my love, why not have Jesus heal you of your aching stomach? Or, perhaps, he can walk across your reflection pool for us." She guzzled down some of the red wine and then laughed boldly.

Some of Herod's friends sitting on the divans with cushions on either side of him joined in the laughter. It was time to ridicule this man from Galilee.

"Jesus, heal me," yelled one of the men sitting there. He along with the rest of the guests were clearly drunk. These were all wealthy men and women. The expensive gowns and robes they wore were exquisite with silver and gold strands running through the material of each.

Judah glanced at every man and woman there in front of him. He calculated that it would take a labourer's yearly wage to pay for just one of these expensive outfits. *Some people had more money than they knew what to do with,* he thought.

The setting was in a courtyard containing many plants and a bubbling water fountain. Flowers bloomed throughout. Cushions were strewn about the beautiful furniture and wooden tables.

Herod and his wife Herodias were heavy drinkers who often indulged late into the night. Their parties which quickly turned into orgies, were legendary. Herod Antipas had a huge sexual appetite that he needed to quench on a regular basis. His lovely wife was fine with this arrangement.

Hence, the lovely young women who were gathered here today along with the men.

One of the young women stood up unsteadily and sauntered towards the prisoner. She walked around him, looked him up and down with a leer, and headed back to her spot on a divan. She practically collapsed onto it.

Smiles were on everyone's faces except Judah Thomas. He was furious. What nerve this woman had. He now understood why John the Baptist had his head sheared off like a rabbit a few years ago.

Once the drunken laughter died down, Herod continued with his questioning, "Jesus, the document from the governor states that you are from Galilee. Therefore, you are one of my subjects. As a subject, I have authority over you. Through the last few years, I have heard wondrous stories about you. You have performed amazing miracles. Many of these so-called miracles took place in Galilee.

I must ask you, Jesus. Are you the King of the Jews?" Herod looked intently at the prisoner before him.

"No. No I am not. I am merely a healer and a spiritual teacher. Caiaphas and his father-in-law just want to see me executed. They fear me," answered Judah Thomas looking directly back at Herod.

The Tetrarch then glanced at the document laying on the table. "Hmm. I have to agree with Pontius Pilatus. I believe you are innocent of any charges. Caiaphas claims you have committed treason and other crimes. The High Priest just wants to see you executed for his own personal and selfish reasons. You have done nothing to endanger or threaten me and my people of Galilee.

I want nothing more to do with this nonsense. I will send you back to the Prefect of Judea now. He can do what he wishes with you. I do believe he will set you free though." He clapped his hands together and two of his own soldiers appeared. "Take this man to the other side of the Fortress Antonia and turn him back over to Pontius Pilatus."

Herod then grabbed his silver cup, and guzzled down more of the red wine as the prisoner and guards left the luxurious courtyard.

Chapter Twenty-Six

Claudia Procula, the wife of Pontius Pilatus ran down the long hallway after her husband. "Pontius, I must talk to you now." With urgency she continued, "I had a terrible dream the other night. It is a premonition that involves Jesus the Teacher."

Pontius, now wearing a formal toga, turned towards her. He absently pulled on the sleeve of the bulky outfit. "Yes, Claudia. What is it?"

Claudia possessed a classical patrician look that made her beautiful. She pulled back some loose hair from her lovely face and said, "The dream was a warning. Jesus has many enemies. In the dream, I saw several evil men surrounding him and pointing fingers at him. One of these men was Caiaphas, the High Priest. He accused Jesus of treason and blasphemy, and said he must die. All these nasty men were yelling at Jesus.

Next, the vivid dream showed a scene where Jesus the Teacher hung on a wooden cross. He was being crucified on this cross that had been pounded into the ground. Several Roman soldiers stood around the cross. A few women and men, family members and friends stood a little further back. They were all crying. The soldiers looked worried and full of fear as they observed the weather. The sky was pitch black and a terrible wind blew. Rain began to pour down on everyone gathered there.

Then, there was a terrible rumble as the lightning and thunder grew in intensity. The lightning lit up the sky. Finally, the ground beneath them shook as a powerful earthquake started. It was horrible to watch.

Husband, this is a warning to us. If you are not careful, Caiaphas and his self-serving cronies will trick you into executing an innocent and kind man. The results will be disastrous for all of us. Eventually, this will destroy your career and you will leave a poor legacy behind."

Claudia, the cousin of the late Emperor Augustus, lifted her hand and stroked her husband's face gently. "Again, be careful, my love."

Pontius nodded his head and kissed her on the forehead. "I have to interrogate Jesus again before I can make a decision. Barabbas, a vicious killer is already tried and ready to be crucified. Since it is the Roman custom to free one prisoner during a ceremony, I will let the crowd decide. Jesus is very popular and I believe he will be freed by the people.

The crowd is gathering below in the small courtyard of the praetorium. Remember, your teacher Jesus is well loved by the people. Do not worry. They will choose him and Barabbas will be executed as he deserves. But first, I need to talk to this Jesus one last time." He turned, headed down the hall, entered a large room and stopped before the prisoner.

The Centurion Marcus and three Roman soldiers surrounded the man. It was protocol for four soldiers to accompany a condemned prisoner to his crucifixion. These four soldiers were there in case the execution took place.

"Jesus, why did Herod send you back to me? I thought he would set you free on his own accord." Pontius scratched his head as he looked at his prisoner again.

"He wants nothing to do with it. He leaves it up to you to decide my fate. He is more interested in drinking wine than taking care of important matters," answered Judah bitterly.

"So be it. You still admit that you are not King of the Jews?"

His prisoner nodded his weary head in agreement.

"You also have not committed any treasonous acts against Rome?" asked the governor.

Once again, Judah turned his head back and forth to answer no. He was tired of the nonsense and wanted it to end.

"Hmm. As is the custom on a holiday, I can free a prisoner as a gift to the people. Most residents here know that. I believe you are very popular and the crowd will want you freed. Barabbas is a vicious criminal and will not be freed if the crowd has its way. Yes, this is the way to proceed. It relieves

148

me of this heavy burden. I can then be free of this mess that Caiaphas and his high priests have created.

This will undoubtedly anger him and his group," snickered Pontius Pilatus. He was extremely pleased with his decision.

"Jesus, follow me onto the balcony of the praetorium to meet the masses waiting below." The governor put his right hand arm out indicating that Jesus was to take his place on the right.

Two of the Roman soldiers pushed the white curtain aside as Pontius walked out onto the balcony. Immediately, the crowd started to yell up. As the twin brother of Jesus joined the governor on his right side, the noise grew a bit louder.

A few moments later, the white curtain opened again and the same two Roman soldiers came out escorting a dirty, bound prisoner between them. Barabbas was a short stocky man with thick legs and arms. Marcus, the tough and experienced centurion followed behind the two soldiers, and Barabbas.

Marcus and his two soldiers were just to the left of the governor, and back a bit. The murderer Barabbas was on Pontius Pilatus's left. The crowd now booed and hissed at this prisoner. He was not liked by the masses below.

Another soldier that had been inside pushed the white curtain back and walked over to where Judah stood. He took up his position behind this prisoner. The crowd was very restless. Some of them yelled up at the governor demanding that he crucify Barabbas. Pontius was pleased by this reaction. It meant Jesus the teacher from Galilee would go free today.

In a private chamber within the Hall of Hewn Stones, the place where the Sanhedrin met, Josephus Caiaphas stood beside his father-in-law Annas. Before them was Simon, the chief spy. The Chief High Priest hefted a leather sack full of silver coins up, nodded his head in satisfaction and said, "Distribute these coins out to the men you have assembled at the praetorium. Make sure they position themselves throughout the courtyard below the balcony. I want them to yell for the release of the criminal Barabbas." He handed the sack to his main spy. "If anyone yells for the release of Jesus, have your men threaten them. 'Give us Barabbas' should be clearly heard throughout the courtyard."

He then motioned with his hands for his spy to go. "Do it quickly, before it is finished. It is a perfect opportunity for us to take advantage of the old custom of freeing a prisoner during a festival."

As Simon headed quickly to the praetorium, Caiaphas said to his father-in-law, "Pontius Pilatus is playing right into our hands." An evil smile was on the face of the Chief High Priest.

He bellowed after his disappearing spy, "Remember to yell 'Give us Barabbas'."

The prefect of Judea noticed something unexpected happening in the mass of people below him. Simon, the chief spy for Caiaphas had just squeezed into the crowded space in the praetorium courtyard. Several rough looking men were around him. He watched as the spy looked down and pulled something out in front of him. The chief spy started handing something out to each of the shady characters around him. Pontius realized the man was giving money to each of them.

Of course, Caiaphas had set this up! The custom of the release of a prisoner by the Roman authorities on a holiday was well known by priests of the Sanhedrin. The High Priest wanted to change the outcome of the event. If enough people yelled, 'Give us Barabbas', Pilatus would have to accept the decision and release the vicious murderer. Jesus would then be executed by crucifixion.

"You sneaky bastard," mumbled the prefect under his breath. He kept watching as the hired men below fanned out through the crowd. It was too late to call for additional soldiers. By the time any of them arrived in the courtyard below, the damage would have already been done. The men paid by the main spy were positioned in key spots within the crowd.

Pontius sighed and then began in Greek, "People of Jerusalem, I stand before you to perform my duty as Prefect of Judea. I have Jesus the Teacher on one side of me and on the left side stands Barabbas, a vicious killer.

As most of you are aware, it is the Roman custom to release, to free one prisoner during a holiday. When I move my hands in motion above my head, I want you to shout for who you want me to release. Shout 'Give us Jesus' or 'Give us Barabbas'. The loudest shout for either of these two men will determine who will be released."

Many of the men below spoke Greek and translated for the ones that did not. Aramaic was the language that they translated the message into. Greek was widely spoken in the Roman world including Judea. In fact, many of the followers of Jesus who came from the village of Bethsaida in Galilee spoke Greek. There was a huge population of Greek speaking residents in Judea and Galilee.

"Alright, remember that Jesus is a teacher and healer, and has not committed any crimes against Rome." Pontius watched the mass below anxiously as the hired men started to push and prod others. "Barabbas is a vicious killer and thief."

He slowly raised his arms above his head. His Roman toga looked impressive.

"Give us Jesus," yelled several men in the crowd below. "Give us Barabbas" could barely be heard initially. Then, the Prefect of Judea noticed wooden cudgels and hard fist being raised towards the supporters of Jesus. The shouting for Jesus lessened and the voices of the Barabbas supporters grew louder. He wished he had time to call in more soldiers but realized any help would be too late.

"Give us Barabbas. Give us Barabbas" filled the praetorium. The cries for Jesus could barely be heard now. A few fists flew to ensure that Barabbas would prevail in this vital contest. Even an occasional wooden cudgel could be seen being lifted by the hired men.

"What a devious bastard," mumbled Pontius Pilatus. The High Priest Caiaphas would pay for this interference.

"Give us Barabbas," echoed throughout the courtyard. The few followers of Jesus brave enough put their arms up in a pleading manner. Their actions were now futile.

Pilatus had now lowered his arms and then used them again to motion the crowd to silence. He yelled, "Quiet." The voices below stopped. "You have made your choice. Barabbas shall be set free."

He looked over at the two Roman soldiers behind Barabbas and nodded his head, "Take him and release him into the streets outside."

The soldiers grabbed the lucky prisoner's arms and escorted him through the archway covered by the white linen clothe. He was walked out of the Fortress Antonia and released accordingly.

Pontius now looked over at the unfortunate prisoner whom he thought was Jesus. "Take this man out back into the minor courtyard. I want him scourged with a whip thirteen times."

The Centurion in charge of the detail raised his eyes in confusion, "Sir, are you sure you do not want him whipped thirty-nine times as is the custom?"

It was believed by Roman soldiers that a man could be whipped thirty-nine times and still remain alive. The fortieth lashing would kill the man. Unfortunately, this was a fallacy. A prisoner whipped could die from the pain and damage at any time. The governor and the centurion knew this through experience.

"I want him whipped thirteen times so that he is bloodied prior to crucifixion. That way, he will have enough strength to carry the crossbeam to the place of execution."

Marcus the senior centurion slammed his fisted arm against his chest in a salute to the governor. Judah Thomas was roughly shoved through the linen covered archway and taken away to receive his horrible fate.

"Oh wait, centurion. I need to place this notice on the wooden beam above his head." Pontius grabbed a writing stylus and inkpot sitting on a table in this private area. He found a scrap of parchment and wrote the following upon it in Greek, Latin and Aramaic: Jesus, King of the Jews.

As the centurion took the notice from the hands of his superior, and started to head after the two soldiers and their prisoner, Pontius gave final instructions, "Do not break his legs. Tie his arms and legs to the wood, do not nail them to it."

Marcus nodded his head in understanding.

In the small courtyard out back, Judah was tied to a whipping post that had seen much action through the years. Remains of dried blood and lash marks covered the wooden post.

One of the soldiers named Felix took off his red scarf around his neck. He headed over to a thorny bush that grew near the back wall. Carefully, he used a knife that he carried on his belt and cut off a piece of thorn. With his scarf, he twisted a piece of thorn into a thorny crown. With a smirk on his slender face, he walked back to where Judah was tied. With great effort, Felix thrust the crown onto the head of the victim. Judah moaned slightly as blood dripped onto his forehead from the newly created wound.

Meanwhile, Sextus, another soldier laughed at this. He held a whip in his hands as another soldier watched. This man was tall and stocky with a wicked scar on the left side of his youthful face. His brown hair was already starting to recede. He was a veteran Roman soldier and had seen lots of action. A hard sadistic streak ran deep in him. He loved being part of a crucifixion detail.

Sextus unfurled the short whip which had small metal balls sewn into the three ends of it. These balls were designed to break the skin of the victim and cause more damage. He snapped the whip to test it. This soldier then looked over at the centurion who had just joined the three of them. He asked, "How many times do you want me to lash the prisoner? Thirty-nine times?"

"No," came the answer. Marcus crossed his powerful arms and continued, "Whip him thirteen times only. I want him to be bloodied but strong enough to carry his wooden cross piece. As per the governor's orders, we do not break his legs. His arms and legs are to be tied to the wooden cross and not nailed."

Sextus did not question his superior. He merely nodded his head and then began the punishment. He brought the whip behind his right side of his body and then flicked it forward very quickly. The three tips of the leather whip snapped and tore through the light coloured robe into the flesh of the victim. Judah Thomas let out a scream.

The powerful Roman soldier continued his task. The second and third lashings tore the flesh even more. The sadistic soldier named Janus smiled as he watched Judah suffering and bleeding. Marcus the centurion felt sorry for the prisoner and knew he was innocent. Sadness filled his brown eyes as he supervised the event.

The robe covering Judah's back became ragged and bloody looking. The screams were loud as the pain wracked his body. Janus took delight in this suffering. His superior noticed this reaction and told Janus to turn away from the scene. He turned reluctantly.

As the whipping continued, Judah lost strength and fell to his knees. Only the hands tied to the whipping post kept him up. Blood and flesh flew everywhere. He moaned and gasped for breath.

After the thirteenth lashing with the short but brutal whip, Sextus coiled it up and held it in his left hand. He took a few steps forward and then ripped off the bloodied cloth that Judah wore. The prisoner was now almost naked except for his loin cloth. All the Roman soldiers laughed except Marcus. Janus had now turned around to view the results. He enjoyed it the most.

The centurion had a dirty red robe laying on the stone floor beside him. He picked it up, and tossed it to Sextus and ordered, "Put that on Jesus, the King of the Jews." At least, the victim would be covered.

Sextus threw the dirty robe over the bloodied prisoner and then untied him from the whipping post. Judah almost fell to the floor. The other two soldiers, Janus and Felix, lifted the victim up, and shoved him over to the corner of the yard where wooden crossbeams stood against the wall.

Janus and Felix then hefted up one of the crossbeams, and positioned it onto the bleeding shoulders of Judah. It weighed over fifty pounds and was a heavy burden for him to carry.

Marcus the Centurion led the prisoner and his detail up some stone steps, out the gates of the Fortress Antonia and into the street. The four Roman soldiers walked alongside the prisoner, two near the front and two just behind Judah. Marcus was in the front on the left side of the victim. It was always tradition for four soldiers to take the prisoner being crucified to the execution site. The centurion always led the way. This method was used throughout the Roman Empire. This had been a time honoured tradition.

Several other Roman soldiers pushed the masses of people back against the walls of the street. They passed another gate that was part of the home of Caiaphas the High Priest. This was where the Sanhedrin and the temple guards had brought Judah originally.

A large crowd had gathered outside in the street. Marcus the Centurion yelled for them to move back, "Get out of our way, you bastards. Move now!" He spoke excellent Latin and then repeated his command in crude Aramaic. This along with Greek were the main languages spoken in this area of the Roman world.

The centurion pushed forward. He was followed by Judah carrying the wooden crossbeam, and the two soldiers, Felix and Sextus. The other soldier now walked behind and pushed people back from them.

"You heard the centurion, you bastards. Out of the way," yelled Sextus as he shoved an old man harshly out of his way.

The large crowd along both sides of the street had grown in numbers. Other Roman soldiers were positioned in key locations ahead of the crucifixion detail. They cleared people out of the way making it easier for Marcus and his men to move forward. Judah staggered along with them. He was getting weaker and had to struggle to keep going.

People were craning their necks to get a look at the bloody spectacle. Some of them were crying, others remained quiet and just watched the scene.

Marcus continued moving ahead with his prisoner and the three Roman soldiers directly behind him. Along the way, a few more Roman soldiers used their shields to create a path and maintain peace in the street. With this many people crammed into this small area, you never knew what would happen. The Romans had a fear of assassins with knives waiting for them amongst the masses. Many a soldier had died this way.

One of the spectators was Judas Iscariot. He leaned against a wall with his hands for support and stood on tip toes. He was shocked by what he saw. Yes, he felt responsible for this horrible event. He felt like a traitor. Utter sadness filled his heart and soul. The weight of the silver coins in a leather sack hidden in the folds of his robe felt heavy, too heavy.

He pushed his way through the people and left the scene. He wandered back through the busy streets. He headed for the temple.

The crowd contained mixed emotions as the Roman soldiers and their prisoner walked slowly along the packed street. Women could be heard crying, some men were cursing the Romans in low voices and a few were jeering at the poor victim.

Judah started to stagger more under the weight of the crossbeam upon his bleeding shoulders. He stopped once to gasp for precious breath before going ahead. He almost fell to his knees but forced himself to remain up.

"Come on. King of the Jews. Keep moving," barked the centurion.

Many of the followers of Jesus moaned and sobbed as they watched the spectacle.

Judah took several unsteady steps forward towards the gate that led out of Jerusalem. This was the outside wall of the city. There were throngs of people lined up in front of this gate and on the other side.

An unused quarry was situated outside. This was called Golgotha, the place of the skulls. They moved as a unit towards the gate that led out.

The centurion swore as the prisoner staggered and then fell to the stone street. Judah was gasping for breath. Some people moaned and cried while others jeered at him yelling, "Jesus, King of the Jews."

Marcus looked around and spotted a large, muscular black man about forty years of age amidst the crowd. His powerful arms were crossed as he gazed at the prisoner with sympathy.

The centurion lifted his right arm which held the short whip, "You. The big man standing there. What's your name?"

"My name is Simon of Cyrene," responded the large, black man.

"Well, Simon of Cyrene. It is your lucky day. You can serve Rome by carrying the wooden crossbeam to the crucifixion site."

Simon of Cyrene looked stunned at the command given to him. "Wha... What are you talking about?"

Marcus stepped towards him in a threatening manner. "Pick it up now, Simon of Cyrene. This is an order. If you want to remain unbeaten, do it now!"

Reluctantly, Simon came forward and bent down. He lifted the crossbeam off the bloodied back of Judah and put it onto his broad shoulders. He adjusted the weight and started forward. The prisoner managed to rise up and follow right behind the big, black man.

They passed through the old stone gate and out into the abandoned quarry. Judah could see two crosses with an upright beam lined-up on a small rocky mound. Two of the crosses were already occupied. The upright beam stood empty between them.

Many people were gathered back away from the scene. The Roman soldiers had put a corridor around the victims on the cross. The soldiers armed with spears and swords stood guard to ensure that no one got too close to the crosses. Again, weeping and many sad noises could be heard amongst the spectators. A few nasty hecklers could also be heard jeering in the back of the gathering.

The centurion and Felix, the first soldier, forced people back, and opened a large area for the condemned prisoner to enter into. The other two Roman soldiers, Sextus and Janus, kept the anxious crowd back along with maintaining an opening here.

"Simon of Cyrene, you can lower the crossbeam onto the ground," instructed Marcus as he scowled at the crowd. "Rome thanks you for your service. Now leave."

Simon did not need to be told twice. He fled the crucifixion site like a rat leaving a sinking ship.

Felix and Janus picked up the heavy crossbeam between them, and climbed onto the ladders that they put onto both sides of the wooden beam. The crossbeam was hoisted up and slid over the upright beam. It went into place securely on this post or beam. A few wooden blocks were fastened into place to make sure the crossbeam stayed in place. Further down the upright beam was a small wooden sitting bench that jutted out a few inches. This was the wooden part used by prisoners to rest their body once in a while. It allowed the prisoner to live a bit longer as he hung there.

Judah Thomas was then hoisted up by the three soldiers of this crucifixion detail as their commanding officer watched. Felix and Sextus tied ropes tightly about the prisoner's arms. The soldier that whipped Judah earlier nailed the notice above Judah's head. The words, King of the Jews, were now displayed here in Latin, Greek and Aramaic.

Marcus the centurion yelled up at his soldiers, "Do not put nails into his wrists or his legs. Pontius Pilatus wants him tied to the cross only." He shrugged his shoulders as if to say he was only following orders.

All the Roman soldiers looked grim and nodded their understanding. They finished by tying Judah's legs tightly to the post. Sometimes, due to lack of wood, prisoners were crucified on the upright beam or post only. No crossbeam was attached. This vertical beam was referred to as a torture beam or post by many.

Janus walked up to his superior after finishing his work and asked, "Just to be clear, Centurion, we do not break the legs of Jesus?"

"Yes. Leave his legs alone. I suspect our governor has a valid reason for doing this." He turned around and eyed the small crowd. The red robe worn by Judah had slipped to the rocky ground beneath his sandaled feet. He picked it up, felt the coarse red material and then flung it aside in disgust.

Family and friends of Judah Thomas were amongst the spectators. The disciple John moved forward and scooped it up like it was a priceless treasure. Meanwhile, his mother Mary, Mary Magdalene, several other disciples from the Capernaum area and Joseph of Arimathea watched helplessly.

The sky became overcast quickly and rain started to fall. A slight wind picked up. A distant rumble of thunder could be heard. Soon, big drops fell onto the parched earth.

The other Roman soldiers who were looking after the other two prisoners being crucified decided to put ladders up onto their respective crosses. Two of them climbed up onto the ladders with their spears in hand. Following their orders given to them previously, they propped their spears behind the legs of their helpless victims. They snapped the weapons in a powerful motion against the wood. The legs of the men were broken. Screams of agony erupted from both of them. The soldiers then broke the other two legs of the prisoners. Again, screams poured forth.

Both of the men being crucified, a thief and a murderer, now had their legs completely broken. This would allow them to die quicker because they could not lift up their bodies and draw in precious breath as before. Their wrists and ankles were nailed to their crosses. These unfortunate men were in extreme agony as they hung there dying slowly.

Judah Thomas glanced over at the prisoner to his right, the thief. The man's face was pale and haggard looking. Tears filled his eyes. Pain wracked his facial features. The man spoke with effort asking, "Why do the Romans not break your legs or nail you to the cross?"

Judah thought for a moment and then replied, "I do not think Pontius Pilatus really wants to execute me. I believe he is hoping to free me later in order to annoy the High Priest Caiaphas. I hope this is so."

"Ah. I hope you are right," said the thief. He then started to whimper as the pain took hold of his body.

When a victim's wrists were nailed onto a cross, the puncture wound would send excruciating nerve pain up the arm. The same result would happen when nails penetrated the ankles of the body. This would create a constant steady pain. Drawing a breath into the lungs would be a struggle every moment. Eventually, the body would not be able to pull in the precious breath. The body would stop breathing and the crucified victim would slowly suffocate. Finally, the heart would slow down and then stop. Death and the release from pain would be the result. Some victims lasted days on the cross. No food or water would be granted. All of this combined into an extreme form of torture.

The Romans may not have invented crucifixion but they had mastered it. It had become the most popular form of execution in the Roman Empire. Only death in the arena for criminals torn apart by savage beasts was the second most popular form of execution.

The wind started to get stronger. It began to howl. The rain increased dramatically. Jerusalem was now in the middle of a full blown rainstorm. Lightening flashed in the distance. Darkened skies above were menacing.

Joseph of Arimathea pulled his heavy cloak up around his chin. As he watched Judah Thomas hanging on the cross, a plan started to form. He noticed that Judah was not nailed to the cross, merely tied to it by heavy rope. As well, his legs had not been broken. Perhaps, if he went to Pontius Pilatus, he could beg for the release of Judah from the cross. Joseph knew the governor and had had several business dealings with him. He believed Pontius even liked and respected him.

Yes, that is what he would do. He would ask for an audience with the Prefect of Judea. Since Judah was merely tied to the cross he could be removed easily. He might be healthy enough to survive.

Nicodemus, his friend and business partner stood beside him. He was also a follower of Jesus. Joseph leaned over and told him what he was planning to do. His friend nodded in agreement.

Joseph also knew Claudia Procula, the wife of Pontius. She had been a fellow student of Jesus in the Garden of Gethsemane at the same time. She might aid him in his quest for the release of Judah believed to be Jesus by the Roman authorities.

The rich merchant from Arimathea glanced at Judah on the cross once and headed back into the city through the gate. Nicodemus went with him.

The storm was raging now. Thunder roared and lightening flashed. It felt like the sky above was at war with itself. Many spectators were superstitious and felt this was a very bad omen.

The wind picked up and became a gale. Many people fled the site seeking shelter as day turned into night.

Chapter Twenty-Seven

Joseph of Arimathea wrapped his cloak even tighter around his chilled body trying to keep the rain out. Nicodemus did the same as he walked alongside his friend. Both of them pushed past the multitudes of people. All of them were trying to seek shelter from the driving rain.

Nicodemus and Joseph kept moving towards the Fortress Antonia where Pontius was staying. Joseph hoped the governor was still in the praetorium where the trial had happened.

Suddenly, the ground beneath their feet rumbled and shook. A large stone wall beside them cracked from the top to half way down its side. They fell to their knees. Joseph grabbed the wall beside him. Nicodemus reached out for the wall on the other side of the street. It felt like invisible forces were after them.

The earthquake kept shaking the ground. Buildings and walls shook about them. Jerusalem was prone to the occasional earthquake. But an earthquake and fierce storm at the same time was freakish. These events of nature would frighten everybody including the Roman soldiers guarding the crucifixion site.

Joseph, a member of the Sanhedrin, took several deep breaths. When the shaking stopped, he and Nicodemus stood up in unison. They continued moving toward the Fortress Antonia. Both of them were soaked through to their skin. Their cloaks hung on them like wet rags.

Nicodemus, a tall, slender middle aged man gathered his strength as he moved ahead. They soon made it to the Fortress Antonia and were let in through the gate. This was the same gate where Judah Thomas had been delivered to the other night.

Claudia Procula stood before her husband Pontius Pilatus. Anger and fierce determination burned from her brown eyes. "Let Jesus go. Free him from the cross, my husband."

Pontius gazed at his wife with love and said, "Once a man is put onto the cross to be crucified, he is not to be removed until his death. That is the Roman custom," he announced this with power in his voice.

"You are the governor of this province. You can do what you wish. You can free him."

"Yes, my love. I know that. But when someone is sent to be crucified that person is not normally released from the cross until he is dead. This would be highly unusual. If Caiaphas the High Priest found out that I released the prisoner Jesus while he was still alive, he would be furious. He might complain to the Emperor in Rome."

"What do you care what Caiaphas might or might not do? You yourself told me he interfered with the trial thereby forcing you to condemn an innocent man.

Husband, you forget that I am a cousin of the late Emperor Augustus. I have noble blood in me. I still have friends in Rome. Besides, what Caiaphas did may even be illegal. Do not worry about him. You are in charge and can do what you wish," Claudia bit her lip nervously after explaining things to Pontius.

The governor was mulling all of this over when a Roman soldier walked into the large room. The man about twenty five with dark brown hair and piercing eyes stopped short of Pontius and his lovely wife. He said, "Joseph of Arimathea and his friend Nicodemus wish an audience with you, sir."

Pontius turned his head and looked directly at the young soldier, "Yes, tell both of them to join me here." He watched as the Roman soldier placed his fisted arm over his chest in salute, turned and headed back to the outer courtyard.

"Hmm. I think Joseph of Arimathea has shown perfect timing in seeking an audience with me now." He smiled, stroked his freshly shaved face and gazed at his wife.

"Perhaps, you are right about everything. I instructed the Centurion Marcus to only tie the prisoner's arms and legs to the cross. On some level, I was already considering freeing Jesus before he died. This would give me the final say and not

Caiaphas. It would be a way to get even with that manipulative bastard.

Yes. I will free him just to spite Caiaphas." He walked over to his desk, sat down on a wooden chair and took out a small scroll. He reached for the stylus, dipped it into the ink jar and then wrote a decree to free Jesus the spiritual teacher. Pontius rolled up the scroll, poured wax onto it and put his seal of his ring to it. It was now officially sealed.

At that moment, Joseph of Arimathea and Nicodemus walked into the large room. Both of them looked like drowned rats.

Joseph nodded his head and addressed Pontius Pilatus who was still sitting at his desk, "Governor, we are here with an unusual request. We were at the crucifixion site, and noticed that Jesus had only his arms and legs tied to the cross. He was not nailed to..."

"Yes. Yes. I am very well aware of this, Joseph. I did not have him nailed to the cross nor had his legs broken. I was contemplating releasing him from the cross before he died on it."

He smiled at his wife and handed the sealed document to her. He addressed Claudia, Nicodemus, and Joseph as he sat there, "Have Marcus the Centurion break the seal and read the decree when you are at Golgotha, the crucifixion site. He will then free your precious Jesus."

Claudia grinned and then kissed her husband on the cheek. She pulled her cloak up around her head, turned and walked towards the two secret disciples. Joseph of Arimathea nodded his head again and spoke, "Thank you, Governor Pilatus."

Nicodemus and Joseph joined her as well as a female servant who followed behind her. All of them headed to the gates of the outer courtyard. Two Roman soldiers opened one of the gates for them. A torrential rain still poured down from the heavens above as they left the Fortress Antonia. They trudged through the wet streets.

The wife of Pontius Pilatus said a silent prayer as they continued through the deluge. She hoped they would be in time to save Jesus. Her servant Maria, also a follower of the Teacher, put a comforting hand on Claudia's shoulder.

The angry sky above continued to punish Jerusalem.

Chapter Twenty-Eight

The site was almost deserted except for the victims on their crosses and a few Roman soldiers. Marcus was amongst them. He had his robe wrapped around his muscular body trying to keep warm and dry.

Mary Magdalene, Mary, the mother of Jesus and a few disciples were also there. They stood nearby in the drowning rain fighting against the steady wind.

Claudia reached in under her cloak, pulled out the sealed document and handed it to Joseph. The member of the Sanhedrin gratefully took the document and slid it under his arm out of the rain.

"Centurion. Centurion," yelled Joseph as he moved towards the cross where Judah Thomas hung. "I have a document for you."

Marcus the Centurion walked towards Joseph and Nicodemus. A slight aftershock forced him to stop in his tracks for a moment. He then continued until he stood directly in front of Joseph of Arimathea. Nicodemus and Joseph had also braced themselves against the slight tremblor.

The rich merchant and secret disciple of Jesus produced the scroll from under his cloak. He slapped it into the hands of the centurion.

Marcus instantly recognized the seal of Pontius Pilatus. He broke the seal and opened the document carefully trying to shield it from the rain. Fortunately, the storm was starting to let up. The rain and wind were less intense. The centurion quietly thanked the gods for this. He carefully read the decree.

"Take the prisoner Jesus down from the cross now," bellowed Marcus. He gave a blistering stare towards two of his soldiers, Sextus and Felix.

As the Roman soldiers climbed the two ladders, and untied the arms and legs of their prisoner, the rain stopped and the sun peeked through the dark sky. A streak of sunlight shone directly onto the body of Judah Thomas.

Everybody gathered there gasped at the sight. The Romans were extremely nervous as they lowered Judah to the wet ground.

A makeshift stretcher made from a ladder was brought forward by Matthew, the former tax collector and John. Blankets were wrapped about the brother of Jesus in order to keep him warm.

"Take him to the Essene healing grotto," commanded Mary Magdalene as she held one hand over her slightly pregnant belly.

Judas Iscariot just barely made it to the Hall of Hewn Stones in the Holy Temple before the heavens opened up. He was protected from the wicked weather by the structure itself. The hall was attached to the northern section of the Temple courtyard. The sturdy stone columns gave him much needed shelter from the storm.

As a small earthquake shook the stone floor beneath his sandaled feet, he placed his hands onto a strong column beside him. The quake lasted but a few minutes. Slowly, he removed his hands from his temporary support. He let his hands hang loosely by his side. A stout rope was hidden among his robe underneath his cloak along with the leather sack containing the thirty pieces of silver. He had come here in bitter despair in hopes of giving the coins back to Caiaphas, the High Priest. He knew the religious official would be somewhere within the Hall of Hewn Stone. The great Sanhedrin consisting of seventy-one members met here on a regular basis.

A few temple guards stood nearby watching him. It was dry within this complex. The roof overhead was supported by numerous columns along the perimeter. He could see a stone throne within the chamber in front of him. Seats made of stone were arranged in a semi-circle before the throne. The room resembled the Roman Forum in the way it was laid out. This was the main meeting room for the Sanhedrin.

Judas noticed some movement across from him. Two priests dressed in expensive robes walked between some of the columns and headed into the chamber towards him. He gathered his courage despite the intense sadness within his heart and soul, and walked briskly towards these two men.

One of them was Caiaphas himself with his father-in-law beside him on the right. They both stopped as they spotted the follower of Jesus heading their way.

Caiaphas raised his eyes in surprise as Judas Iscariot rushed forward screaming, "I do not want your blood money." The depressed disciple of Jesus pulled the leather sack out and threw it at the High Priest. Many of the silver shekels rolled onto the pavement. Torch lights nearby caused the coins to glint.

Two temple guards stepped towards the very angry man. Caiaphas simply shook his head to say no. They stopped with hands on the hilts of their swords.

Judas yelled, "You sneaky bastard." He turned and ran past some columns out to the edge of the temple courtyard. The rain was pouring down.

Annas, the father-in-law of Caiaphas and former High Priest merely glanced down at the beautiful silver coins, and said, "We can use these silver shekels to buy Potter's Field. That way, we will have a graveyard to bury the poor and unknown."

Caiaphas nodded his head in agreement.

Judas Iscariot ran along the edge of the courtyard under the roof supported by the many columns that surrounded it. He exited the temple out an archway and rushed into the street. He looked at the turbulent sky above, raised his fist in anger and cursed God.

He kept running down the street and turned into a narrow alleyway. The tight alley was not much wider than a foot path. He stepped out of it onto a very wide street. On the other side, a low stone wall ran along the street. An old dying tree stood next to the crumbling low wall.

Judas pulled out the stout rope. A noose had already been made at one end of the rope. He tossed the other end of the rope over a low hanging branch of the ancient tree. Carefully, he tied this end tightly onto the branch.

He cried, took a deep breath and released it slowly. "It is my fault Judah Thomas died. I should not have listened to the Master Teacher. People will hate me for betraying him."

The tears could not be seen through the pouring rain as he put the noose around his neck. He tightened the noose, sobbed and then stepped off the low stone wall. His neck was snapped like a twig instantly. His sandaled feet dangled, and swung back and forth.

The soul of Judas Iscariot had left this mortal earth.

Chapter Twenty-Nine

They laid Judah onto a wooden table in the middle of the Essene healing grotto. Several niches had been chiseled into the rock walls.

These niches contained clay and wooden jars full of medicines. Mallow, willow bark, lavender, ginger and stinging nettle were all stored here. Even the poppy seed pain medicine could be found amongst the many medicinal jars.

This healing grotto was one of many found in the land. The Galilee and the area near Jerusalem held several of these healing places. The Essenes had operated the healing grottoes for a few centuries now. It was a great service that the Essene sect provided for the sick and wounded. A sick person could receive treatment here administered by an Essene healer. All were skilled healers and herbalist.

The person receiving a treatment could also stay in a room of a home nearby. Food and drink would be provided for them. There was no cost associated with this. Donations were gratefully accepted.

This particular grotto where they had brought Judah was very large. Two extra rooms had been cut into the rock. It was very comfortable here. Stone benches, wooden chairs and tables were spread throughout this huge grotto.

Some of the stone floor was covered with animal skins and rugs. Blankets, pillow and drinking water were also kept here. Linen clothes, bandages and wooden splints were stored here as well. Medical instruments were kept on a wooden table nearby. These instruments included saws, knives, forceps, tweezers and other items.

Sometimes, a patient needed an amputation of a leg, arm or hand. The various saws contained inside the leather bag on the table were used for this very reason. In fact, Jesus and Judah performed surgical amputations a few times over the years in the same manner as Greek physicians.

It was cool and comfortable in this healing place. Judah lay on the table drifting in and out of consciousness. Blood dripped from his mouth and nose. His breathing was laboured.

"Help me turn Judah over onto his side," commanded Jesus as he stepped into the healing grotto and lowered his mantle from his head. "I need to look for damage on his body."

Mary Magdalene, John, the youngest male disciple and Agnes, a friend of the family, turned the badly injured man onto his side.

Jesus looked at his brother's back and carefully examined the ribs. He gently touched the wounds created by the short whip used by the Roman soldier. He shook his head slowly. "A few of his ribs have been cracked, some may even be broken. He is suffering from internal injuries. I fear some of his organs have been damaged. This type of whip used by the Romans can prove fatal in some cases."

The mother of Jesus and Judah put her hand on her eldest son's shoulder. "Can you heal him? You have healed the blind and the sick many times. Surely, you can heal your brother too," tears were in her eyes as she finished speaking.

"I do not know, mother. His internal wounds may be beyond healing. I fear one of his organs may be too greatly damaged." He shook his head sadly as he glanced at his brother's bruised and bloodied back.

He, along with his wife Mary, placed his brother flat onto his back gently. He prepared a pain relieving drink and then carefully poured it down his injured brother's throat while Mary held his head up slightly. Judah mumbled, opened his eyes and then shut them again. He whispered, "I have seen heaven. It is beautiful. Our father waits for me there." He looked like he was in agony as he finished speaking. He shut his eyes again.

Jesus along with his beloved wife Mary skilfully cleaned and wrapped the wounds of their patient. Judah's breathing became less laboured and more rhythmic as the poppy drink took effect.

"Everyone, lay your hands on my brother's body. We need to send healing energy to him. This is all we can do along with praying for his recovery," Jesus commanded as he laid his hands onto the chest of Judah.

His brother had now lost consciousness for several moments. His breathing was very slow. Mary Magdalene checked her brother-in-law's pulse by touching the neck. She shook her head slowly, "His pulse is very weak and slow. This is not good." Tears filled her beautiful eyes.

John the youngest disciple laid his hands upon the stomach area of Judah Thomas. Simon, the former fisherman and man that denied his friendship with Jesus was now there in the spacious grotto. He put his large hands onto the shoulders of Judah. Mary Magdalene lovingly placed her delicate hands onto the head of the badly injured man.

Even Joseph of Arimathea who had joined them at the crucifixion site with the decree from the governor laid his hands onto the feet of Judah Thomas.

In a moment, the healing energy from all of them entered the battered and severely injured body of Judah Thomas. This energy that they all channeled into the body came down from heaven above and flowed through all of them.

Judah's breathing became very slow. He was now in a deep, unconscious state: he was almost in a coma. Mother Mary put two fingers to his neck to feel the pulse: it was very slow and weak. This was not a good sign. Finally, Judah's breathing became even slower with several moments in between each breath.

Jesus noticed a mist starting to form just above the abdomen of his twin brother. The mist slowly expanded over the top of the comatose body. It took the shape of Judah but was ethereal like a fog. The soul of Judah Thomas was now floating just above the physical form. Jesus could make out the facial features of his brother clearly on the ethereal face. The eyes were shut as the soul floated like a gentle cloud above the physical body.

This ethereal form that was the soul of Judah Thomas now floated up away from the physical form. It then slowly went through the ceiling of the healing grotto. A cord of misty white light which was attached from the stomach area of the body went up to the back of Judah's soul. This white cord slowly unraveled and then completely disappeared like fog vanishing under the rays of the sun.

Everyone present noticed that Judah had stopped breathing. Many of them started to cry as they realized he was dead. Even the strong masculine Simon, the former fisherman had tears streaking down his bearded cheeks.

The eternal soul of Judah Thomas, twin brother to Jesus, had now left the earthly realm and returned to the heavens above.

Chapter Thirty

Mary Magdalene, Mother Mary, Jesus and Agnes, a loyal follower, prepared the body of Judah in the healing grotto. They washed the blood and dirt away, anointed the body with oils and then wrapped it lovingly in linen cloth, completely covering it from head to toe.

The body was then carried by several of the disciples including Simon, his brother Andrew and others out of the healing grotto, through the gate, and onto the dirt pathway. A stone fence surrounded the healing grotto, and contained a small garden with beautiful flowers and plants within its interior. Many of the Essene healing grottoes throughout this area and into Galilee were designed in this lovely manner.

The garden tomb belonging to Joseph of Arimathea was nearby. They quickly moved the body of Judah Thomas to this private tomb that was built into the native rock. An outer courtyard of stone greeted them. They went straight towards the door. A large round stone was attached to the wall beside this doorway. The shape and size of the stone would make it easy to roll it in front of the open doorway. It was several feet wide and taller than a man's height. It measured about fifteen inches wide.

Inside the rock tomb was a burial niche on the right. Simon, Andrew, Matthew and the others placed the lined covered body onto this niche that had been carved out of the rock.

Mary Magdalene, Mary, the mother of Judah and Jesus, Agnes, and a few other women stood outside in the stone courtyard: all were crying softly.

The men left the rock tomb of Joseph of Arimathea. Simon, a huge bear of a man, along with his brother Andrew and Matthew rolled the huge round stone into place sealing the body of Judah within the rock tomb.

Joseph of Arimathea standing by himself just within the courtyard said, "I will go to Pontius Pilatus, and ask that his soldiers keep the curious and spectators away from the garden tomb and the healing grotto."

Jesus who was quietly observing everything from behind his mother and his wife, stepped forward. "We need the Roman soldiers to roll this huge, round rock away tonight. We must move my brother's body out of the tomb and make arrangements for it to be taken to Nazareth. We can then bury him in a private tomb near our home. It will be a secret site similar to the one we provided for John the Baptist, my cousin.

We will leave some linen sheets on the burial niche in the tomb of Joseph of Arimathea." He smiled over at his friend and student. Joseph nodded back.

"This way, the tomb will be empty and the Romans can tell people that he must have risen from the dead. All of you here, especially the ladies can go forth and proclaim this miraculous event.

I am sure Pontius Pilatus will be fine with all this. After all, his wife Claudia Procula is a follower of mine. He is also wanting revenge on the High Priest for his trickery.

I know you have just rolled the round stone into place in front of the tomb but it needs to be rolled back again, please," Jesus smiled at the disciples who were still catching their breaths and recovering from the exertion.

"Simon, Andrew, Matthew and John, please make the necessary arrangements to transport my brother's body back to Nazareth. My younger brother Joseph who is at home knows where we can bury Judah in secret. Allow him to set it up."

The sun shone brightly on the red hair and beard of Simon, the former fisherman making it glow. All of the disciples nodded their understanding. The stone in front of the tomb was rolled back again and the body of Judah was removed. They placed the body carefully on the ground of the courtyard. With some effort, the huge, round rock was rolled back into place again. Only some linen cloths were left inside. All four of these disciples along with a few others took the body to a horse stable nearby. A wagon was obtained for them to transport the body of their former teacher and friend back to Nazareth.

"I am sorry to hear that Jesus is dead," said Pontius Pilatus as he washed his hands in a marble container. He poured more water from the pitcher over his hands again. A servant handed him a white cloth. Once he was satisfied that his hands were dry, he ordered the servant to leave. He glanced at the equestrian ring on his middle finger. This showed his status as an Equestrian, just below the senatorial rank.

"My dear Claudia and Joseph. I did my best to help Jesus in this terrible trial forced onto me by Caiaphas. What a treacherous and manipulative man. I made sure that Jesus was only whipped thirteen times and not any more. I ordered my centurion to tie his hands and feet to the cross. No nails were used and his legs were not broken.

When Claudia approached me, and then you and Nicodemus, I agreed to remove the body whether it was alive or dead. I fear the metal balls at the end of the soldier's whip did terrible damage to the internal organs of your teacher Jesus. This is not the first time something like this has occurred.

Once again, I am sorry. I will have my soldiers keep the masses away from the rock tomb and the adjacent healing grotto. My soldiers will roll the huge round rock away from the tomb in the middle of the night. As you stated, Joseph, they will only find some linen cloth lying on the burial niche within.

My men can state that the body has miraculously disappeared. They can start a rumour that hints at Jesus being risen from the dead.

Yes," Pontius rubbed his long nose absently. "Yes, this will work. It will anger and frighten Caiaphas and his father-in-law to no end."

A slight smile graced the face of the Prefect of Judea. Both Joseph of Arimathea and the wife of Pontius thanked him, turned and left the reception chamber in the praetorium. A few song birds could be heard singing somewhere in the distance.

Chapter Thirty-One

It was a gentle and beautiful spring day. The Galilee was tropical in climate and always had warm weather. It had a rainy season and a dry season. Sometimes, the days could grow fairly warm but today was different. It was the perfect temperature.

Jesus stood on the green mount near the Sea of Galilee. This was the very same spot where he had given the Sermon on the Mount. He had remembered that his brother Judah had written down the sermon and made copies. These had been passed onto several of the disciples. The sermon beautifully described what heaven was like. People still talked about it even to this day.

Matthew was also an unofficial scribe for the organization. He was responsible for recording the events that occurred in the Galilee, the healing of the blind and crippled, and much more. Many lectures by the Master Jesus had been written down by Matthew, the former tax collector.

This guaranteed that the spiritual work of Jesus, his brother Judah Thomas and the disciples would be kept alive for future generations.

Jesus, the Master Teacher and healer gazed about at the people gathered before him. His beautiful wife, Mary Magdalene, stood beside him radiant with the glow of her pregnancy. Her belly was starting to show the signs.

Simon and his brother Andrew stood quietly in front of him, just a few feet away. Joseph of Arimathea, dressed in a rich cream coloured robe, was beside the mother of Jesus, his hand lightly on her shoulder.

Several other disciples and followers had gathered here. All seemed happy with a few of the female followers smiling.

The Master Teacher smelled the wonderful breeze, pulled his hair back from his face and said in Aramaic, "It is a blessing having all of you here today at the very site where I gave my Sermon on the Mount. The eleven remaining disciples are here as well. This is very important.

I will be asking all of you to spread the word, to spread my message of love. You have all been taught the laying on of hands and how to use herbs for healing. Allow these skills to be used when needed on others. Gather in plazas, homes and open forums. Speak to the masses about heaven above and our eternal souls.

I am hereby giving all of you the authority to baptize the people in my name, in the same manner that my cousin John baptized the many."

The warmth of the Galilean sun and a breeze from the Sea of Galilee greeted all as they stood or sat there in front of Jesus.

"It is paramount that we form groups of people into spiritual communities in cities throughout the Roman Empire. I am asking all of you, especially my close disciples, to make this your mission. God is love and this message must be spread to the masses. Teach people how to heal using the ancient techniques that the Egyptian healing centers employed. Provide food, clothing and shelter for the needy in places that you have established communities."

Simon interrupted, "Are you going to allow your wife to do the same work that the male disciples do? They should keep to healing and herbs, and leave the spiritual teaching to the men. That is the way it has always been."

"Simon, my friend, my wife will be teaching to the people in the same manner that you and all the other disciples do. Both male and female followers will be able to do this work." The Master Teacher looked at his disciple in a stern but kindly way.

"What! I should be allowed to teach as one of the leaders of our movement. Mary should not be able do this. It is wrong," protested the former fisherman.

May Magdalene stepped forward and put her hand onto her husband's arm to keep him quiet. "I will be a teacher and leader within our group. I have as much right as you do to teach the masses, Simon. You will not stop me."

The face of Simon turned red with anger upon hearing this from her. He shut his mouth and decided to discuss this with

Jesus at a later date. He did not want to make a scene in front of the others gathered here.

Jesus started to speak with authority again, "In a moment, all of you will receive a gift from God above. A great energy will pour through the tops of your heads and enter into your bodies. You will feel wonderful with this amazing energy as it flows through you bodies. Your psychic and spiritual gifts will unfold. You will become great healers, teachers. Many of you will be able to see the human aura around people. Angels and spiritual beings will communicate with you giving you wisdom and knowledge. Prophetic visions, and enlightening dreams will guide each and every one of you. You will also be able to soul or astral travel out of your bodies and visit people at a distance. You can heal others while in your soul form when you astral travel. Some of you may be able to visit heaven and communicate with loved ones passed over. All of you will develop key gifts that are yours.

Now, I want all of you to close your eyes and then lift your arms up towards heaven. Ask that the energy from God comes to you. Take in a deep breath and feel this powerful energy entering through the top of your head."

All gathered had their eyes closed and their arms raised up to heaven. Soon, the energy from above poured into all of them. Each disciple and follower became covered in white and gold light. It completely surrounded all of them. Smiles of pure joy were on the faces of everyone. Then, the light disappeared, and all the followers and disciples lowered their arms one by one.

"Open your eyes now. You have all been initiated and are ready to enter the world. You will be ambassadors of God. Many of you will perform miracles and help the masses. Blessings shall flow to all of you, my friends," Jesus stopped talking for a moment, gazed at everyone, kissed his wife on the lips and then continued, "I miss my twin brother Judah Thomas. He gave his life to save mine. Thankfully, I have some of his writings that he left behind."

Some of the followers, especially Agnes, were crying softly at the mention of Judah.

"My dear friend and disciple Judas Iscariot followed my instructions, and brought the temple guards and Roman soldiers to the Garden of Gethsemane in order to arrest me. As we all

177

know, my twin brother took my place. This allowed the event to play out as needed.

He felt guilty and depressed over the demise of my brother Judah, I believe. He probably blamed himself for it.

Judas Iscariot was a loyal disciple and friend. I will miss him dearly. He served a great purpose and followed my desires. He was not a traitor although history may make him into one.

We are gathered here today to discuss our future. I want all of you to go out into the world and do the same as I have done. Heal the sick, comfort the poor and form communities."

Jesus now glanced over at his student and supporter, Joseph of Arimathea. "My wife Mary and I will be travelling with my dear friend Joseph of Arimathea to Southern Gaul. We will continue to heal and preach to people. We will form a spiritual community there."

Joseph, a member of the Sanhedrin smiled back at his teacher. He gave the mother of Jesus a gentle pat on her shoulder.

A soft breeze blew in from the Sea of Galilee. The palm trees, flowers and green grass bathed in the warmth of the sun above.

"Tomorrow," Jesus announced, "We will all leave to different cities in the Roman world to spread our message and provide healing to the needy." He opened his arms as he finished speaking.

The blue of the sky and the sea greeted everyone. Perhaps, this was a sign of a wondrous future, a future where love and peace filled the world.

Chapter Thirty-Two

Jesus the Master Teacher lay on his deathbed in a secluded bedroom at the Essene Mystery School of Mount Carmel known as the School of the Philosophers. He was a very old man.

From Mount Carmel, Jesus had overseen his organization and advised his many disciples over a period of almost five decades.

Matthias, the grandson of Matthew, the former tax collector and disciple, sat in a chair beside the bed of Jesus. He kept his writing materials nearby on a table. A sad smile lay upon his young bearded face as he gazed at the ancient face of Jesus. The beautiful blue eyes of the Master looked back at him. Those eyes were still as bright and penetrating as ever.

"Matthias, my young friend and disciple, try not to be so sad," Jesus smiled and laughed. "After all, everything of this earth has its own cycle. Death is merely a continuation of life in a higher form."

"But, Master," exclaimed Matthias in an anguished voice. "We will miss you dearly."

"Remember what I taught you, Matthias. There is no death. There will never be. Our human souls are eternal and directly linked with God. It is the physical body that we reside in temporarily while we are here on earth that dies. We are souls with bodies, not the other way around. When our physical form can no longer house our soul, we vacate the house and vibrate to a higher energy, and return to the heavenly fields. While up there, we rest, review that life and receive special instructions. When we are ready, we return to earth where our soul enters into the body of a soon-to-be born child. We repeat this process again and again until we learn all our lessons here on the physical plane of existence." Jesus lifted his right hand and placed it on top of his young disciples' tightly clenched hands.

"Do not worry. We will all be together again in heaven and on earth in future lifetimes."

Matthias seemed to gain strength from these words. He unclenched his hands, and gently squeezed the Masters' hand in his and then sat back in the chair. He placed his hands in his lap. "You have asked me here. I came as soon as I received the message."

"Yes, I am pleased that you are here. My time is limited and I must discuss certain concerns with you of events in the past. The manuscript that your grandfather wrote is wonderful but it is not enough."

Jesus had to hold back the tears as he thought of his close friend and disciple of many years. "You must realize that my teachings are based on ancient teachings from Atlantis and Egypt, and are to be used as a spiritual way of life. The Essenes follow this way. It is not a religion and should never become one. I hold great fears regarding this!"

The young man looked down at the Master in a knowing way. Matthias started to think about the changes that had happened in his own lifetime. He knew Jesus' fears were not unfounded. "I know that you speak of Paul of Tarsus and others that have perverted the true teachings in the past."

The Master's still handsome face wrinkled up into a grimace as he replied, "Paul irked me greatly. He twisted my teachings and my sermons although he meant well. He had a dislike for women and relegated them to secondary positions whenever he could. He influenced many men in key offices to turn my organization into a patriarchal system. The teachings, the words should have been spread by both men and women. Many of my own disciples have been women. God or the Creator is a supreme being consisting of both male and female principles. Both energies are necessary to manifest life."

Jesus shut his eyes for a moment and focused on his laboured breathing. His life energy was slipping fast. He opened his eyes again and continued, "I want you to record this and the following story I am about to relate to you. Your memory is excellent, Matthias, so you can simply listen to my tale now. Later, after I have passed on, you can put my words into writing."

Matthias glanced quickly at his now abandoned writing materials and leaned forward in his chair giving the Master his full attention.

Jesus took in a deep but hesitant breath into his struggling lungs and began, "I wish to discuss the so-called crucifixion and resurrection. I feel somewhat burdened by it all."

His young disciple raised his eyebrows in surprise. "Why would you feel burdened by this miraculous event?"

The Master Teacher raised his right hand with effort motioning his young friend to silence.

"When I was thirty-five years of age, and into my fourth year of teaching and administering, a dangerous situation arose. The Great Sanhedrin and other powerful men were jealous of my influence on the populace. These men wanted me dead and sent spies to watch my every move. A conspiracy was formed to manoeuver myself and my inner circle of twelve disciples into Jerusalem at Passover. Their intent was to have me arrested and tried for blasphemy. My crucifixion would have been the result.

Joseph of Arimathea, a member of the Sanhedrin, was a sympathetic friend to our teachings. With great risk to his own life, he met me secretively near the village of Bethany and warned me of this conspiracy.

All of us, including your grandfather Matthew, sat up late into the night and discussed our options. We were gathered in a circle by a grove of olive trees with a small fire in the center. It was Matthew, in fact, who came up with the solution to our grave problem. He suggested that my twin brother, Judah Thomas, could help us. The only discernable difference was that Judah had brown eyes not blue ones."

Jesus stopped talking and gasped for breath a few times. His eyes were shut and his face looked contorted. Finally, he gained his composure. "Anyway, it was decided to use Judah as my impersonator for a while, as he had done in the past. My brother with the same spiritual persuasion as myself was approached with the idea. He wholeheartedly agreed to help us. Unfortunately, the plan went awry during Passover.

It was my twin brother who was arrested in the garden of Gethsemane on that night so long ago. Poor Judas Iscariot in fear of his own life and in an attempt to protect me, identified Judah as the Master with a kiss upon his cheek. When Judah, who was believed to by myself, went before Pontius Pilatus, the prefect reluctantly condemned him. Pilatus was not fond of the Jews and especially the Sanhedrin, but was tolerant of my teachings. He did order his Roman soldiers not to break the legs of Judah in hopes of removing the man from the cross before death set in. This Roman official may have been cruel to some but for some reason, he had a certain respect for the gentle Essenes and their way of life. As well, his wife Claudia Procula was very interested in my teachings and believed in God.

When Judah was crucified in my place that day, there was a minor earthquake and a terrible rainstorm that arose. While this horrible event was unfolding, both Nicodemus, a disciple of our group and Joseph of Arimathea approached Pontius Pilatus in private, and begged the release of their Master from the cross. Claudia Procula was present as well. Pilatus quickly assented their request and passed a hastily prepared reprieve to these two men.

Due to the powerful storm and earthquake, very few people were left at the site of the crucifixion. Some of my followers, my mother and Mary Magdalene were present. A Roman centurion who was sympathetic to us was standing nearby the cross. Joseph of Arimathea thrust the document into the centurion's hands. From that point, Roman soldiers removed my brother from the cross. Some of my disciples along with my wife, wrapped him in linen and carried him away to the Essene healing grottos nearby. My brother was still alive at this time. The Roman centurion remained at his post. He told any curious onlookers that came by that Jesus was dead and had been taken away to be buried in a cave belonging to Joseph of Arimathea."

Matthias sat back in his chair and gasped in awe at Jesus. The small room was silent for several seconds. Only the occasional sound of birds and the wind blowing gently through the trees outside the bedroom window could be heard.

The Master commenced with his story again, "Sadly, my brave brother Judah did not recover his ordeal. Pontius Pilatus sent soldiers to the burial cave owned by Joseph of Arimathea.

People were kept away from this area for three whole days. Finally, on the third day, after my so-called death, Mary Magdalene and some others who were privy to the secret, arrived at the burial cave. The Roman guards had already rolled back the huge boulder a few nights previously exposing an empty tomb. Only some linen cloth was inside laying on the burial niche. Mary Magdalene and the rest of them went out into the public proclaiming that Jesus had risen from the dead. Soon, word spread throughout the land, much to the consternation of certain members of the Great Sanhedrin."

Jesus started to gasp for air again, curtailing his amazing story. He shut his blue eyes and lay there struggling for life giving breath to enter his lungs.

Matthias turned his attention away from the face of Jesus and gazed out the window at the stone wall that encircled the huge complex. He watched as a black bird descended and landed on the wall. He started to search his memory wondering what a black bird meant.

Using his great clairvoyant ability, Jesus, who could not see the wall, spoke up, "Matthias, they say the sighting of a black bird foretells of death. Upon that wall sits a sign. It is my omen. When it flies away, my soul shall fly away also."

Darkness was starting to descend upon Jesus. With a final effort, he spoke,

"I miss my beloved Mary Magdalene, and my two children and many grandchildren. All my old friends and disciples have long since gone. I feel sad and alone. I have lived, loved and cried. I have lived a wonderful and full life. My old body feels like a grain of sand upon the desert floor. With the coming of the wind, I will vanish from the land into the distance." A single tear rolled down his cheek. His eyes had a faraway look. "Promise me, Matthias, to record all of what I have said."

He closed his eyes and murmured, "Mary, I loved you so. How I missed you. It is time for me to go." Jesus let out one final breath and his body went still.

Suddenly, a beautiful white light appeared at the foot of the bed and soon the shape of the archangel Michael formed from this great light. He held a golden sword in one hand while his other hand reached out for the soul of Jesus the Master. At the same time, a white light arose from the body of Jesus now known as the Christ and moved towards Michael. This heavenly and powerful messenger started to shimmer, and turned once more into a magnificent white light and became smaller. Both these illuminations moved about the room together and then exited through the bedroom window heading towards the black bird perched on top of the wall.

Matthias, the grandson of Matthew the former tax collector and disciple, gazed out the window at the apparition of death. Two swirls of white light danced together and moved towards the black bird. The bird flapped its ebony covered wings and lifted up into the sky. The brilliant white lights joined it in its ascent. All continued to gain height climbing towards heaven. Soon, the wondrous spectacle was lost to Matthias' eyes. The black bird of death along with its special companions had flown into the heavenly fields.

The soul of Jesus could see all of his loved ones and friends waiting for him in a beautiful garden there. The flowers and trees were breathtaking. The soul of the Master Teacher had come home.

Suggested Reading

De Long, Douglas. *Ancient Healing Techniques.* Woodbury, MN: Llewellyn, 2005.

Ancient Teachings for Beginners. St. Paul, MN: Llewellyn, 2000.

Past Lives for Beginners. Woodbury, MN: Llewellyn, 2014.

Lewis, H. Spencer. *The Mystical Life of Jesus.* San Jose, CA: AMORC, 1937 (reprinted in 1965).

The Secret Doctrines of Jesus. San Jose, CA: AMORC, 1937 (reprinted in 1965).

Pagels, Elaine. *The Gnostic Gospels.* New York: Vintage Books, 1981.

The Gospel of Judas. Washington, DC: National Geographic Society, 2006.

Prophet, Elizabeth, C. *The Lost Teachings of Jesus: Missing Texts, Karma and Reincarnation.* Gardiner, MT: Summit University Press, 1994.

Reincarnation: The Missing Link in Christianity. Gardiner, MT: Summit University Press, 1997.

Ward, Kaari et al., ed. *Jesus and His Times.* Pleasantville, NY: Reader's Digest Association, 1987.